SPEAKING THE LANGUAGE OF THE UNIVERSE

HOW TO MANIFEST YOUR DREAM LIFE

SIMRAN MOHANTY

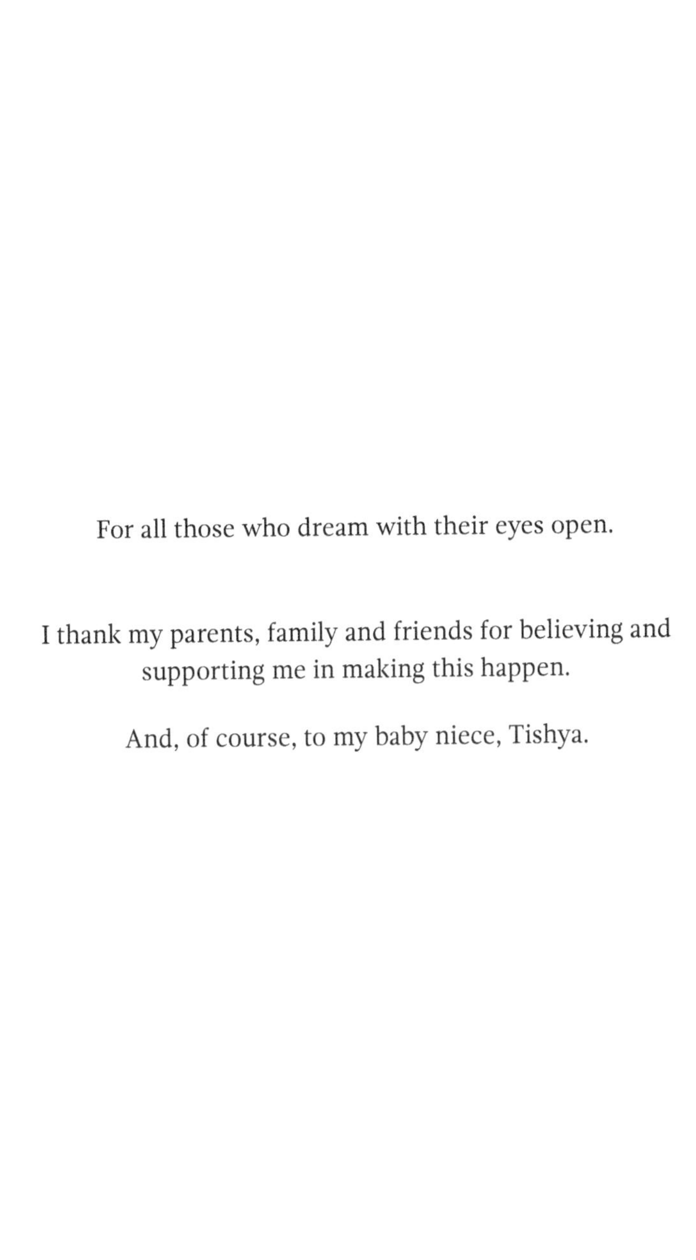

For all those who dream with their eyes open.

I thank my parents, family and friends for believing and supporting me in making this happen.

And, of course, to my baby niece, Tishya.

Contents

Contents

Introduction

Observe.

Observe the world around you. Observe life. Observe yourself.

What have you been missing out in your life thus far?

You don't have to answer that now. That's the job of this book to get you your long-awaiting answer. This book reveals ways to dig into your highest self and manifest your deepest desires. You'll soon discover how to call for abundance in terms of health, money, relationships and life.

You didn't choose this book; it chose you.

My intention for this book is to share my belief and knowledge with humanity.

I, for one, always wanted to write. I manifested my way out to become a professional writer. Still, writing and publishing a book seemed like a dream—in just 90 days!

But yes, what I had in me was the drive and the confidence to make it happen and Voila!

I won't go on and on boring you, telling you about my life and its other unneeded information. But the whole point lying underneath: if I can transform my dream into a reality, so can you!

Achieving greatness isn't impossible–provided you're ready to break walls, push boundaries and unleash the unthinkable.

Do you feel a little "J" when you see your neighbour's BMW flying straight in front of your face, when your colleague won that big fat lottery or when your cousin cracked the NASA interview? It could be anything you really want but can't have in your life. But, there is magical power inside us to make it ours. You don't have to be chosen or lucky; you just have to explore this power called *manifesting*.

I see people around me who wish to manifest money, career, life partner, happiness, and peace. It hasn't worked out for some of us because we're still a step away from understanding the connection between the Universe and us.

Again, *"Rome was not built in a day."* It'll take a reasonable amount of time, proactive efforts and calming patience to navigate toward them.

However, this book isn't promising pesos, palaces, or paradise. Apologies already! Though, I hope and pray you have it all.

But guess what? The journey and the knowledge you walk out with will be worth it. You'll have the confidence to make significant changes in your life. You'll be able to deal with troubles more calmly, worry less and above everything, be self-confident, happy and a better human. Isn't that what we aspire for at the end of the day?

Keep turning the pages of this book to get the most out of it and your life. This book has one primary objective: to break down the meaning of manifestation into bite-sized, digestible bits and allow your dreams to evolve.

And yet, don't push for things to happen. The more you force things your way, the more you scat them away. Instead, open up and surface your desires. And I'm going to show you how. This book will be your guide.

Thank you for coming on this journey with me.

So, turn the page!

How To Use This Book

Okay, to get you the most out of this book, let's talk about what each part of this book holds for you.

There are a total of five parts here, namely, the five W'S: Wish, Write, Weave, Welcome, and Win. Each part is then further divided into five sub-chapters. If you do the math, 25 chapters stand in the way between you and the life of your dreams you manifest. Here's what each part will teach you:

Part I: Wish

As the name suggests, this is where you look into uncovering the hairline difference between a dream and a wish. This'll also zero in on the law of attraction and what it entails. Following this, you'll learn about the manifesting tools we're going to deploy throughout our journey. And finally, this part unveils what goes behind well-set intentions, high frequencies and vibrations and how do they intertwine.

Part II: Write

Throughout this part, you'll find writing exercises to hone your scripting skills toward the end of the chapters. There isn't anything to be overwhelmed or scared of. This part will make you believe that you can manifest pretty much everything in your life just by writing.

But, for the Universe to notice your written affirmations, you need the secret ingredient: gratitude. Plus, it has a couple of techniques and guidelines sprinkled, which, when governed, will accelerate your manifestation quotient in no time. Who are you? What is your reality? Get your answers here.

Part III: Weave

Reaching this part of the book means you've completed 50% of it, so kudos! As the name denotes, this part teaches you to weave the fundaments of manifestation we've learned so far. It demonstrates why inculcating the right habits in our life is crucial. Know more about how to wreathe the virtues of meditation into our mind, body, and soul. What actions have been missing from your life? How can they lift your life for good? Unearth them here.

Part IV: Welcome

To welcome a new tomorrow, it's vital to let go of the limitations and the past that you've been clinging to for too long. When you're ready to embrace change, you hint to the Universe that you're prepared for the magic to unravel. Accept positivity in your life with open arms, steer away from negativity and fear, and have forgiveness in your heart. What are the biggest fears trapped inside you? How do you let go of them? This part has your answers.

Part V: Win

And finally, you're in the last part of this book, congratulations! This part unmasks the nuanced differences that'll help mark a definite impact on our lives. It'll answer why some things didn't work out in our favour so far and how we make it happen now. This will also tell you why giving your all and living in the present is quintessential to seeing your dreams come true. With that, you're all set to manifest; you're manifesting-ready!

Each of these 25 chapters has a little "DIY Exercise" to sharpen everything you've learned so far. Every chapter builds from the last one. This is then followed by a P.S section, also known as "Please See." It ensures that you're guided by tips and tricks on applying these exercises to your personal lives, helping you take the desired steps to reach your goal.

This is a self-help book and to see a difference in your life that is worth your time, efforts and energy, commit yourself to its chapters and learnings. Start practising these DIY exercises sincerely and implement them into your life.

This is your opportunity. Seize it!

Are you ready to get started?

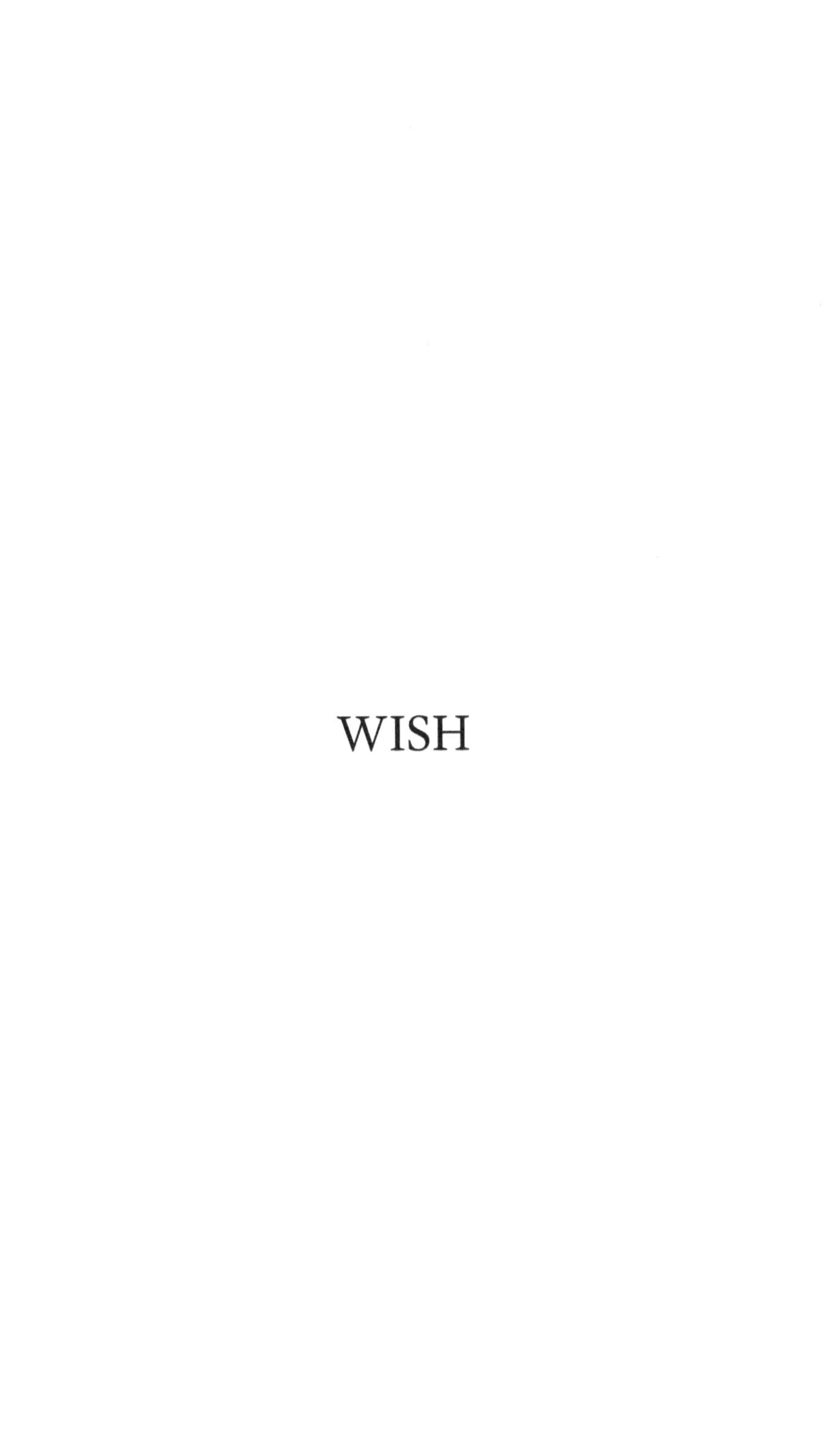# WISH

CHAPTER ONE

DECODING DREAMS

Have you ever thought of the mechanism behind dreams? Why do you see them? How do they occur? And what are they trying to tell you?

Through your subconscious mind, your dreams try to communicate with your conscious mind. As your conscious mind slips into a state of rest, your inner subconscious mind takes over. It then decodes your deepest wishes and naked fears.

All you have to do is tap into your subconscious mind and let it unfurl deeper significance. Your dreams truly want to emerge through you only when given a chance.

You dream for a reason. They choose you.

It is simple–dreams are thoughts.

And these thoughts shape your mindset. What you think (your thoughts) and what you feel (your emotions) produce energy that magnetises your experiences. It is the origin of our intention and the point from where our reality begins to emerge through.

The situations you're in, the people you're around and the outcomes you experience are a part of how you think and your thought process works. The thoughts harbour in your mind and convert into physical reality.

Open yourself to the world of imagination and play with your thoughts. Believe in the possibility that you'll attract all you want. Say it out loud,

"My thoughts create my reality,"

"I am what I think,"

"I am empowered."

When you start to fuel your thoughts with positive emotions and the right actions, they gain weight of their own and become more powerful, thereby allowing us to dream bigger.

What you dream of now is a tiny part of the manifestation process. There lie several hidden layers of beliefs underneath them.

Initially, you might find all of this too sceptical, especially to have a staunch belief in something you can't see, hear or touch. There will always be a certain level of doubt holding you back from whether or not the whole thing will work out.

But don't let that stop you from dreaming.

Pursue your dreams.

Start paying attention to what you think and what you dream. Soon, you'll see the invisible line of connection between reality and dreams. You'll find another medium of communication with the Universe from your dreams. And you shall be able to connect the dots.

What if I say everything you've always wanted was just a thought away?

It just needed you to give it a little nudge and manifest it in the right order.

There is a triangular connection between your dreams, manifestation and the law of attraction. The latter of which we'll learn in Chapter 2. Even though it sounds somewhat surreal, you'll soon realise that you can manifest the life of your dreams, *easily.*

The real secret to manifestation lies in deciphering what you truly want.

Ask yourself what you want in your life. Say it to the Universe and grant permission to co-create with it. Soon, you'll have all the answers within yourself that you've been looking for your whole life. You'll start to feel the difference and gain all that you once desired.

The quicker you grasp the true meaning of manifestation, the easier it will be to translate your dreams into sheer reality. Trust yourself and let the magic surprise you.

Grab yourself a notebook and pull a chair. Let's get you a quick Do-It-Yourself exercise.

DIY Exercise

To begin with, take a deep breath and start visualising what you want to manifest. Think of it this way: you have a magic wand and a globe of insurmountable power in your hand. Neither can you be defeated nor can you go wrong. Allow the power of imagination to seep through you and think of all you want in your life right now.

Ask yourself—what does the life of your dreams look like? Do you want a new job where your boss appreciates your efforts and doesn't nag you? A promotion that you deserve and have been waiting for years? A supportive spouse with whom you can grow old? A seven-star villa? A car? The list could go on.

List out five such things that you want in your life right now. Arrange them in order of priority, placing your biggest wish at one and so on.

1.

2.

3.

4.

5.

P.S: Remember, this is a free space. There is nothing like too much or too little. Expand your capacity to believe in yourself. What you choose for yourself now will firm an establishment on which everything else is built on.

So, dream big!

CHAPTER TWO

THE MAGICAL LAW OF ATTRACTION

You could debate that you tried every idea, technique, or theory out there to sail in the direction of your dreams. You did everything possible under your control to make progress. Yet, somehow or the other, things didn't go as planned and you hit rock bottom.

Let me assure you; that it's completely normal. However, at this point, it is crucial that you don't be tempted to go into a self-critical mode and doubt your self-worth. It's now time that you understand what went wrong and stopped you from fulfilling your wishes.

"What you think, you become.

What you feel, you attract.

What you imagine, you create" - *Buddha.*

Identifying why you haven't lived the life of your dreams yet is what you need to ascertain in your manifesting journey. Although it might seem impossible to discern the reasons now, the process is much simpler than you think.

The law of attraction is simple and this is what it preaches:

"You are powerful. You are worthy. The Universe is ready to accept your orders."

The key here is honesty. Be brutally honest with yourself. The techniques and ideas in this book will work out in your favour only if you want them to. Unless you don't believe, enjoy or appreciate this journey, you might as well miss out on the beauty of this experience. All that this book asks you is to *try*. That's all.

Try to imagine a scenario where:

You get paid to sleep.

The innate purpose of sleep is to strike a balance between our brain and body. It allows your mind and body to recharge, leaving your refreshed and energetic when you wake up. As humans, we need a minimum of six to seven hours of sleep a day to maintain a healthy lifestyle.

But what if I told you there is a new inventive way where you get paid to sleep? Simply put, you generate a new source of income; just from sleeping.

What would you do now? You'd make it a point to carve a few hours from your hectic schedule to sleep, right? And let's face it, who doesn't like sleeping?

What makes this process so easy? The fact that you love it? Or that you don't *have* to do it yet make extra money?

Similarly, the magical law of attraction helps you attract what you want while you enjoy the process and without making it sound like a mundane chore.

It functions this way–you ask and it is given. The Universe wants what you want.

It states that everything in the Universe vibrates on its own frequency. And things with mutual frequencies resonate.

In short, if you ask for positivity, you seek positivity. If you ask for negativity, you seek negativity. No puzzle there. Hence, trust the process and get reciprocated with fulfilled wishes.

DIY Exercise

Think about these three questions:

1. Which wish would you like to see fulfilled in the next 12 hours?

2. Which wish would you like to see fulfilled in the next 12 months?

3. Which wish would you like to see fulfilled in the next 12 years?

For example, you could begin with, *"I would want to pass my entrance test with flying colours in the next 12 hours," "I would want to meet my soulmate in the next 12 months,"* and *"I would want to have a healthy family, parenting adorable kids in the next 12 years."*

The point is to feel good about these wishes and seek it from the Universe to co-create these changes. Know that change is the only constant. The raw state of the Universe is change. Don't be afraid to be a part of the change you once feared. Affirm that the law of attraction will give you the strength to tackle this change.

Ask yourself now:

"What makes me truly happy?"

"What feels good to me right now?"

"What is it that is yearning to emerge through me?"

P.S: Look for commonalities in your answers. And know that there is no right or wrong answer here. So, believe in the magic of the law of attraction and let it charm you.

CHAPTER THREE

MANIFESTING TOOLS

Now that you have a fair idea about manifestation, dreams, and the law of attraction, it's time to scale up your knowledge and help you get the most out of it. This chapter will unveil some of the most accessible tools to simplify the manifesting process. Let's see what we've got here:

- A Manifestation Journal

From now on, start documenting and mapping all your thoughts, dreams, goals, plans and desires in a journal. You might as well grab a piece of paper and pen to note, but creating a separate journal will keep track of your answers and expressions. This will make the process more special and motivate you to keep documenting your journey.

Also, when you write things out, you magnify your intentions and become more aware of what you want. Writing produces energy that reaffirms your manifestations better with the Universe, more of which we will learn in Part II of this book.

Treat this journal as a sacred space where you're away from judgement, inhibitions, and fears. It's exclusively yours!

Additionally, you can also rely on this journal to record the answers present in the DIY Exercises of this book.

- A Vision Board

You've already painted a picture of what your dream future looks like. But it's still in your head.

How do you ensure you act upon it and turn it into a reality? A critical aspect of manifestation is reassuring yourself by visualising everything you want to see in your future. Visualisation is one of the most effective brain workouts you can begin with.

If you're more of a visual thinker than a scribe, you can start putting up images, words, quotes and drawings that match your dream. It's always better to create a blank canvas only for posting your affirmations. Else, you could paste these on your wall, wardrobe or nightstand–anywhere within your regular line of sight.

But first, believe in the power of a vision board.

Be specific about what you wish to visualise. Then look for sources that can form a collage of these positive affirmations–images, words, quotes and drawings. Build, maintain and interact with this collage daily; that way, you stay reminded of your dreams and goals.

Vision boards have been proven to be an excellent manifestation tool as it helps you organise your intentions and boosts the chance of making things happen.

- Trust

How is trust a manifesting tool now, you ask?

Yes, this is something you already have; you just weren't aware of using it as a tool until now. This is one such manifestation tool that begins with yourself. You need to trust the Universe and believe that it has your back.

Steer away from apprehensive questions like:

"What if I'm just wasting my time," "What if this process is just in my head," and "Can I really receive what I want in my life just via manifesting?"

While that holds, remember it is a fair exchange of trust and support. If you think that all I have to do is write my affirmations on a vision board and then the Universe will do its job–I'll have to stop you right there.

Think of it as an even trade where you do your bit, the Universe does its and together, you'll facilitate the future of your dreams.

Trust the flow of life and don't be afraid to let go of your inhibitions. Once you start relying on the natural laws of the Universe, you'll find how things begin to favour you.

As you make peace with trusting the Universe unconditionally, you tend to stay aligned and rooted with your dream–despite any external circumstances.

Then comes the point where you don't have to push to bring your dreams into being. You open up to the Universe and allow it to interact with you. Soon, you'll find plausible concurrences to bubble up only because you were expecting them to.

- Commitment

You'll have to commit yourself to the process to experience the newer reality and the new you. Promote a steady commitment to this book's learnings, lessons and exercises to see the best results.

You've begun to dream about what you want next in your life, what you want to manifest in life. Now, the Universe, too, holds a vision for you. It's like you take a step, and so does the Universe until you both meet halfway. But yes, affirm yourself by saying:

"I will take the first step."

DIY Exercise

It's 'DIY-o-clock,' and it's time to keep track of what we've learned so far with this chapter. You can use the given space below to chart your answers or utilise the journal you've created for this purpose. Alternatively, you may opt for other versions, such as Word or Keynote as well, if that helps.

Name five things currently happening in your life that you're happy about.

    1.

    2.

    3.

    4.

    5.

For example, you may write about things like:

"The Amazon voucher that I received from my last transaction," "The visit to Thailand last summer," "The ideal employee I hired last month that I had been looking for months," "The little black dress that I was gifted last birthday."

Choose one of these happy statements and write five words or phrases that resonate with your pick.

    1.

    2.

    3.

4.

5.

For example, if it were me and should I have chosen "The visit to Thailand last summer," some of the words that I would have picked would be: *"Family time," "Great Thai food," "Break from work," "Excellent sight-seeing,"* and *"New people and culture."*

P.S: You'd have noticed that these exercises ask you to write things down. The more you write your dreams down on paper, the more you sync with an unseen connection with the Universe.

That is precisely what these manifesting tools help you with—stepping closer to your dream.

Remember, happiness starts with little things and it is all around you. You just have to learn the art of appreciating and following it.

Perhaps a trip to Thailand wouldn't be a big deal for some people. But acknowledging and writing down even the trivialities like Thai food and culture will bring you happiness. The Universe, too, wants you to find happiness.

Usually, the first words or thoughts that come to your mind are the unaltered, genuine ones. Hence let your imagination speak.

Go for it!

CHAPTER FOUR

ENERGY, FREQUENCY AND VIBRATION

Just like Science has laws such as "Newton's Laws of Motion" or the "Laws of Conservation", the spiritual part of the Universe too has its own laws. The primary principles of understanding these universal laws lie in their inter-relation to "energy", "vibration", and "frequency". Let's decipher its interaction with one another.

- **Energy**

New age spiritualism tags the law of attraction as a pseudoscience. Basically, pseudoscience is a belief deemed both methodical and fictional yet cannot be proven scientifically as it lacks evidence.

This belief relies on the concept that thoughts emanate from "pure energy" and that positive thoughts attract positive energy while negative thoughts call for negative energy.

The physical reality around us is a result of how our senses interpret the energy of what we experience.

When we start pulling positive thoughts and feelings into ourselves, our body draws energy that has the power to magnet positivity in life. Our energetic vibrations produce signals to the Universe that attract and send similar signals back to us.

We align toward the frequency of the reality we've been "thinking about". This is how the Universe works too. This means that when you pursue your dreams, the Universe receives this energy and wants to co-create with you to turn this into a reality. What actions you take and the amount of dedication you channel toward your dream makes the difference, something which we'll be learning in Chapter 15 of this book.

You are made up of energy,
So are your thoughts,
As are your intentions.
In fact, the Universe exists because of energy!
And we feel it because everything that is made up of energy vibrates at a certain pace. This brings us to our next topic, vibration.

- **Vibration**

Everything in the Universe is built up of atoms that are constantly vibrating. Even though you wouldn't be able to see it, it happens.

Just as the law of attraction preaches that our intentions originate from the power of thoughts, the law of vibration also originates from the power of feelings. Our intentions don't gain weight until we tap into the vibration associated with our thoughts.

Every time you think through your subconscious or conscious mind, your body exudes a chain of reactions that change your vibrations, making you realise how you feel.

We can significantly transform our manifestation practice by bringing conscious awareness to our feelings. One of the first things in manifesting is to strike a similar-ranged frequency to the things we're trying to attract.

You'll realise that you have the power to attract wishes that harmonise with your vibration. And that's why you attract people who are in harmony with your vibration and don't "connect" with people where this vibration is missing.

As they say, *"like attracts like"*.

For instance, when you meet someone new, you may say things like, *"I liked her vibe"*, or *"Our vibes matched"*. When you *vibe* with someone, it technically means that your vibration is on a similar frequency to theirs. "Vibes" is the "Gen-Z" term for the vibrations that we're referring to here.

Your emotions not only influence what you want to manifest in life but also signify the vibration that you're currently in–positive or negative. To fulfil your manifestations, you'll have to tune in with the current vibrational patterns of your life.

A stable frequency of your emotional awareness will help you sail toward your destination. This brings us to our next topic, frequency.

- **Frequency**

Take a second from whatever you're doing and ask yourself the following:

"How do I feel?"

And don't categorise them into the "good" or "bad" bucket. Technically, you can't always feel either "good" or "bad". Sometimes you may feel ecstatic, elated, anxious, surprised, jealous, or even indifferent. You feel anything beyond just good or bad. All your feelings are legitimate and charged with high or low frequencies.

Higher frequencies attribute to positive emotions like joy, happiness and enlightenment. Lower frequencies, on the contrary, attract negative emotions such as fear, guilt, and shame. The goal is to raise our vibrational frequencies, blocking out the negativity and attracting only the positivity.

The second you start operating from a place of high anxiety, dread, fear and insecurity, you invite negativities around you. This then starts reflecting on your feelings.

You start to doubt your self-worth: *"Am I even good enough for this?"*, *"Can I do this?"*, *"Why is my life like this?"*

Remember, all feelings are valid. There is nothing like a right or wrong feeling. In every moment, you have the choice to feel anything you want.

However, before you master manifestation, know how to decipher your real feelings.

Ask yourself:

"Are these my real feelings or are they forced upon me?"

"Are my feelings valid?"

"How do I stay true to myself?"

DIY Exercise

Pick your favourite time of the day, when you're away from distractions. Steer away from your phone, tablet, PS6 or even your dog. Take 15 minutes from your schedule, allot this exclusively for yourself and label that as "Me

Time".

Now, close your eyes and imagine you are in the lap of Mother Nature and all you can see around is verdant greenery. All you hear is the melody of birds chirping. You are slowly tapping into serenity, calmness, and a happy state of mind.

Start to talk to yourself about your true feelings.

"What am I good at?", "What is the most important thing in my life?" "Is there anything in my life that I'm truly happy and grateful for?" "What feelings do I want to bring into my life?"

Doing this exercise will help you talk to yourself. Reflect upon your thoughts and introspect deep within you. People might think this is crazy, but if you want to unlock answers deep inside, it begins with you.

Look around and establish what brings you joy. You could find happiness in eating your favourite dish, talking to your friend after ages, or even watching your favourite show (in my case, *FRIENDS*)!

It varies from person to person. It's crucial to be aware of your inner feelings. That's when you enter the special high-frequency moment and can attract all the positivity you want.

Vibrations are powerful.

Trust them and make space for them.

The entirety of the law of attraction works only when you intend to manifest positive energy, enhancing your vibrational frequencies to meet a higher version of yourself.

When you've identified that you're truly happy now or in a high-frequency moment, you've raised your frequency to attract goodness. That is precisely when you've got to make a wish for your manifestation to come true.

Say it out loud:

"I am truly happy, energized and in the flow".

"I can see my dreams getting fulfilled".

"My wish is coming true."

P.S: This exercise is about owing up to one's true feelings. If you're not in the best state of mind, admit it, and there's nothing wrong with that.

Manifestations rely on our feelings and energy. The more you empower it to dwell in your head, the higher the chances that the Universe will transform it into a reality. The stronger the output of your frequency, the higher the quality of the attraction you receive.

CHAPTER FIVE

SETTING INTENTIONS

In the last chapter, we've surfaced the connection between energy, frequency and vibration with the law of attraction.

You're now aware that you create your reality. You're responsible for your beliefs. You're the maker of your own life.

Now, you're in a stage where it's time to follow your dreams and convert them into reality.

Your dreams are the sincerest form of your desires. Your thought process is a combination of emotions, beliefs and awareness. That's how thoughts form a base from your true intentions to evolve. Drawing a clear frame on what you're calling in life is the next step we will to delve into.

The first ingredient for a successful manifestation practice is setting up a clear intention. Intentions you intend (subconsciously or consciously) are the ideas you wish to manifest.

Simply put, what you intend is what you manifest. Your thoughts, in the rawest form, manifest your reality.

Think about it this way:

"I am successful in my career",

"I have a loving and supportive spouse that I always wanted",

"I am debt-free and financially secured".

Such thoughts emancipating from your inner self will allow the Universe to co-create and give you a chance to make it happen. Now compare it to the following sentences:

"I am no longer in a toxic relationship", "I don't think I have what it takes to crack the interview", or something as simple as *"I want to be happy in my life".*

You see the differences here–each of these phrases lacks positivity.

What you think is what you manifest.

If you set up a clear intention and ask the Universe to grant you positivity, it surely will. And if you're apprehensive about the process and let negativities dwell within you, how will Dear Universe get a chance to co-create with you?

Also, while setting up intentions, it's always better to think about it in the present tense instead of the past.

For example, you could re-word these scenarios as:

"I am no longer in a toxic relationship" to *"I am in a respectful, happy relationship now."*

"I don't think I have what it takes to crack the interview" to *"I am confident about my skills and the interview."*

"I want to be happy in my life" to *"I am happy in my life."*

And don't go hard on yourself when it comes to specifics. If you don't have a specific timeframe or a checklist for your intentions to succeed–that's fine.

Then again, don't limit yourself while you're in this stage. You must allow yourself a bigger room to dream, paving the way to the doors of possibility. You'll have to give wings to your envision for it to translate into a reality. If you limit yourself here, how can the doors of possibility open up?

The best part about setting intentions is its fluidity. It's limitless, open to change and based on your beliefs. They originate from your thoughts, whether you consciously feel them or not. And like your thoughts, your intentions surface reality only when you fuel them with determinations, conscious actions and, of course, a firm belief.

DIY Exercise

Mention three things that you desire right now. It could be anything from playing with your kittens to cooking up your favourite chicken noodles to buying an apartment. The trick is to keep the list to a maximum of three on a priority level. The more desires you set intentions on, the power to achieve them diminishes.

1.

2.

3.

For this exercise, time yourself for sharp 30 seconds: no less, no more.

The idea here is to filter only those desires that you intend to have in your subconscious mind. The more time you take to complete this list, the higher will be your urge to edit, deprioritize, pause and essentially go crazy.

P.S: Here are a few tips to help you with this exercise:

• Don't limit yourself. Think big!

• Stay positive with your thoughts. Try to steer away from negative thoughts like "I can't", "I don't", or "I won't". This will only pull your energy down.

• Keep the list to the point. For example, if you have an important document stuck in the courier and you've not received it yet, affirm yourself by writing, *"I am getting my document and I am feeling delighted about it."*

When you start writing down your affirmations, you send the Universe a vibe that you're ready to manifest–something I had previously mentioned in this book. In the next chapter, we will take a deep dive into the science behind writing, the related techniques and how it helps accelerate the manifesting method.

WRITE

CHAPTER SIX

POWER OF WRITING

What if I told you that you could achieve your dreams just by writing?

What if I told you that you could script your wishes into reality?

What if I told you that the adage, "Pen is mightier than a sword," is scientifically proven?

Although it might sound surreal, the short answer here is YES!

Once you begin writing your wishes, dreams and desires in a pen and paper format, you strike an intimate connection with the Universe. By inscribing your thoughts down, you activate your imagination. And the raw mental images in your mind start to form a captivating scene.

Your brain is the centre of all neurological activities. The connection formed by your brain, hand and pen allows you to pull in power that accelerates your manifestations to come true. Subconsciously, you trigger your brain to send off high-frequency signals to draw things toward you.

Science claims that the human brain uses the same veins for imagination as it does for carrying out the task in reality. This simply means that the more you engage in visually painting a picture of your manifestations in your head, the more you make-believe your brain as if you're doing it for real.

When you start penning your thoughts, dreams and wishes, this generates energy that helps in matching reality to your vision. When processed with a clear intention, these focused thoughts allow the Universe to manifest for you.

The whole point of writing your goals is to remind you of the wishes that you desire to manifest. This technique is referred to as *scripting* in the manifestation dictionary. By journaling your wishes, you create an ideal outlet to feel, express and leverage your gratitude to the Universe.

The power of writing or scripting helps in bridging this gap.

It lets you to observe your current reality and enforces a regular pattern in your mind by writing it down. When you draft your manifestations, the Universe notices your newfound efforts and begins to do its part to correspond to them.

DIY Exercise

Of the tools mentioned in Chapter 3, we've learned that a manifestation journal is a must-have tool throughout your manifesting journey. When you start journaling the details of your day, aspirations or the DIY exercise of this book, you're already halfway through building your dream life—just by writing.

Let's get you into the practice of writing.

Identify a habit that involves writing you do every day. It can be an email that you write to your manager, a text to your friend, or even a post-it note on your refrigerator for your kids. Now, you want to fuel your writing habits to something bigger and deeper.

I am a writer and this is what I do for a living–I write. But for those who aren't in the writing business, writing might be profusely tricky, especially when not in a habit.

Here are some tips I pass on to my clients who ask me, "How do I start writing?"

The answer I give is—just write.

Don't worry about the description, details or grammar too. The task here is to get you into a habit of writing. Even though it might seem hard at first, with practice, there will come a time when you'll rely on your journal to express your true feelings.

For example, I started writing about the things I liked. I love food (who doesn't?) and began writing blogs and articles on food and travel. Since I was already into writing, I added it all to my website.

As beginners, you too, can start writing about things you like. Exploring the globe? Mountaineering? Gardening? Dancing? It could be anything that interests you. Pick that in your journal and cook up a story.

P.S: Remember, you don't have to write for the editorial or the newspaper. You are writing for yourself. Write words that make you feel at ease, and you'll start enjoying the process sooner than later.

Backing intention by words empowers your affirmations to enter a zone of awareness as a message. This brings us to the next chapter that will decipher how to manifest our affirmations just by writing.

CHAPTER SEVEN

CONFIRMING AFFIRMATIONS

Now that you have got into writing, it's time to learn the subtle art of confirming your written affirmations. But first, what are affirmations?

Affirmations are short statements empowering positive thinking and boosting encouraging self-esteem. It fosters a belief you can achieve all that you want, provided you have the drive. For affirmations to spin their magic, ensure they are positive and to the point in the present tense. Here are a few examples of positive affirmations:

"I am good at my work."

"I am strong, powerful and happy."

"I am getting better every day."

Repeating affirmations pave the way for positive thinking and assure the Universe that you have taken a step further from setting an intention. This gets retained in your brain and signals the Universe that you're ready to surface the reality you once manifested.

The difference between writing a journal and affirmations is that you're now reassuring yourself that you already have all you had once planned to manifest. This is how our brain works; if you can stay positive and charge in persistence even through the battling times, your brain makes it feel real.

The more concise you get with your affirmations, the more powerful they turn. As mentioned earlier, the three main components for an active affirmation are: it needs to be in the present tense, positive and to the point.

- **Why present-tensed affirmations?**

Writing your wishes with a present tense, such as "I am....", "I have....", "I can....," serve as a vibrational reflection to the Universe that you already are or have or can.

Even though they haven't been physically manifested yet, your mind and soul receive a message that they have, thereby amplifying their chances of coming your way.

Regardless of the nature of your dream manifestations, writing them makes the result more magnetic. Try to begin your sentences with words like:

"I am thankful for ....."
"I am excited for ......"
"I am satisfied for ......"
"I am grateful for ......"
"I am happy for ......"

Now you may choose to write these in your journal, the traditional pen and paper format, but if you want to continue the same with an online format, that's fine too. I prefer writing it down, as the satisfaction of writing your wishes down instead of typing them out is more reassuring.

- **Why positive affirmations?**

The Universe makes things happen only when you use positive language in your ask. Positive thoughts have higher power than negative ones. Just a minute of pure positive thoughts in a day can transform your life tremendously.

You might wonder if saying things like *"I am not sad"* and *"I am happy"* mean the same thing. Technically, you're right, but the Universe doesn't understand this language. It does not respond to negative annotations like "not," "don't," or "can't."

Start inculcating positive sentences in your life aside from the dreams that you choose to manifest, and you'll see the stark difference. Remember, there is always something positive around the corner happening to you; you just need to see it.

Think of the following situations:

"I am unhappy with my job as I have this gruesome boss who is a jerk."

"I have utterly scornful flatmates who pry into my business."

"I didn't like the taste of my burger today. It was way too salty."

If you could relate to any of these situations, the very thought might rile you up with frustration. But, before that, take a minute to see what you missed.

The Universe gave you an opportunity, something to feel grateful for. Instead of looking at the obnoxious presence of your boss whom you dislike, be thankful that you're at least employed when so many people around you work so hard to get a job. You would find many people in your circle who are tirelessly trying to land a job offer.

Similarly, you can also be grateful for the money the job provides you. It's no surprise that people crib about their respective jobs–it's a universal thing. But what matters is to rise above it and to find beauty even in an ugly circumstance.

Now, when you think of the second example entailing nosy flatmates, try to see what you're missing out on. Be grateful that you can hear. You have a roof over your head and a house to head to after work. Even though I hate to say this, many people don't have some of the above.

And the same goes with the third example as well. What matters is that you have no scarcity of food around you. You'll find people around you who find it difficult to put food on the table. Also, a burger can be a luxury for some. Therefore, try to see the underlining beauty that is often taken for granted.

- **Why to-the-point affirmations?**

The more you tend to be specific about your desires; the Universe finds it easy to give you precisely what you manifest for.

For example, if you say, *"I am happy,"* the Universe will find ways to make you happy but had you given something more specific like, *"I am happy to finally get married to the man/woman of my dreams,"* the Universe will work toward finding you the right partner. Now, it is more aware of your intentions and knows exactly what you want.

Similarly, instead of saying, *"I am a millionaire,"* try something specific like, *"I make?10, 00,000 a year"*. The more specific you get, your chances of feeling your visions increase.

DIY Exercise

Write a letter to yourself about the things you're happy about. Time yourself for 15 minutes to do this exercise. Grab your journal and start writing.

Mention the things that you feel thankful for. Remember to write in the present tense, with positive words and don't be afraid to go 'to the point' too. For example, this is a sample letter you could write to yourself. Pay attention to the language and the scripting here:

"I am truly happy that I finally found a job that I had been looking forward to. I feel so good that I'm earning independently. I get to do a job that I'm truly passionate about. Plus, I get to work with people I love.

Every passing day, I get to be better at my job and my zeal to deliver more increases. All my hard work and efforts have finally paid off. I have finally landed my dream job. Thank you, Universe. Thank you for all the fulfilment and happiness. Thank you for all the love; I enjoy every second of my professional life."

See what you did here?

You imagined yourself in a positive part of your life, in the present tense and to the point. Your ability to vividly describe every detail makes it possible for you to envisage this just like a reality. You allow yourself to experience the exact feeling as if this were truly happening to you.

P.S: You're more powerful than you could ever imagine. And now, you're triggering the Universe to join hands with you and co-create the dream you've always wanted. All you need is a sense of gratitude to welcome these with open hands—which is what we'll learn in the next chapter.

CHAPTER EIGHT

EXPRESSING GRATITUDE

So far, this book has taught you about the undeniable power of the Universe and how steering in the right direction can help manifest the life of your dreams. The more you appreciate life, the more you realise how much you have to live for.

"What you appreciate, appreciates" - Buddha.

You might have heard a lot about appreciating what you have in your life, but have you given it an honest try?

Imbibing positivity in what you seek fetches you more wonders than you initially sought. And to unlock these wondrous results, you need one key: gratitude.

Take a moment to stop worrying about whatever you're dealing with in your life. Instead, use this moment to appreciate what you already have. A second worth's time of gratitude is a second well-invested in pulling your manifestations closer to you.

There is a thin line between "a thing of wish" and "a thing of gratitude."

When you wish for something, you tell the Universe that you don't have that and indirectly reaffirm that you have an incomplete desire. On the other hand, a mere expression of gratitude pulls your desires to start surfacing your reality.

It is a human tendency to get agitated when life doesn't go as planned. You wanted to watch your favourite movie, but the stupid traffic made you miss out on the first part. You asked your date out, but you got stood up. You cooked pasta only to see it getting burnt.

Getting negative thoughts and drawing in negativities is only human; trust me, it's okay!

I won't be saying that having a vein of frustration in your head is unnatural. Instead, try to zip through these circumstances by filtering out the negativity and attracting positive energies toward you.

Zero in on the positive side of life and feel the warmth of gratitude–that's how gratitude magnifies.

Be grateful for the small things in life. Remember, you start small and then you'll be able to see the bigger, brighter light. For example, think of a pleasant memory that brought a smile to your face. It could be:

• Your application for the manager's position was approved!

• Your brand-new pair of sunglasses!

• You finally learnt how to make circular tortillas!

• You slept for complete 8 hours yesterday!

You might be wondering, where is the big deal? This happens to everyone.

Of course! But what doesn't happen to everyone is getting a feeling of enlightenment from these little things in life. And that's what this book teaches you.

A slight sense of gratitude for the small things can change your life drastically in a short span. Once you start doing it, you'll soon begin to relish life and feel how easy and enjoyable it is.

And believe me, this emotion is within you, something that is easily accessible to you. Let's get you into a quick DIY exercise to help you access this emotion.

DIY Exercise

It's time to pull out your journal again. You can use the given space below to complete this exercise too.

This exercise needs to be done toward the end of the day when you're finally done with your work and off to sleep. Mention five things that happened in your day that you're grateful for.

You can begin with five, but if you have a few more delights that took place in your day, feel free to add them too. You'll soon have much to add to the list, which is excellent!

1.
2.
3.
4.
5.

P.S: When mentioning the things that made your day, take a couple of seconds, say 30, to feel the warmth of gratitude in your heart for each of these items.

For example, your office conducted a seminar today and you had a chance to be one of the speakers.

Think of the podium, adore the fact that you were the centre of attraction for the whole audience. If you had stage fright in your childhood, you finally overcame that.

Allow your mind to connect with your heart truly.

Let's now decrypt four great techniques, when deployed, can bring you a step closer toward your dream–by writing.

CHAPTER NINE

TESTING TECHNIQUES

Of the many techniques used to manifest, the following four have been my personal favourite: the 369 manifestation technique, the 55x5 manifestation technique, the pillow technique and the two-cup technique.

These are one of the first exercises I discovered when I was new to the law of attraction and to the concept of new age spirituality in general.

Theory behind 369:

Serbian inventor Nikola Tesla coiled the numbers 3, 6 and 9 as the "divine numbers". His theory linked the magnificence of these numbers to the keys of the Universe.

So, why only these numbers and what do they signify?

• 3 symbolises our connection to the mighty Universe.

• 6 symbolises our inner strength and harmony.

• 9 symbolises our inner rebirth (which means letting go of what no longer serves us and changing into who we are becoming).

Affix your intentions to one particular wish. It can be anything ranging from a well-paid job to getting married soon.

Next, grab your journal and a pen. You'll need them to follow this technique. You'll be following this technique for the next 33 days.

Here is the trick–we're going to maintain writing our manifestation for a minimum of 17 seconds. No, I haven't picked it out from thin air; there is a logic behind it.

Research has it that the power of holding an affirmation for 17 seconds helps connect our mind to create the energy of the thought we focus on. For instance, if we focus on the thought of a brand-new car for 17 seconds, our brain starts to create more energy, aligning us to what we're claiming.

Now, the steps:

Step 1: Note down your affirmation 3 times in the morning.

Step 2: Note down your affirmation 6 times at noon.

Step 3: Note down your affirmation 9 times in the evening or night.

Here is an example of what you might write:

"I am having my business take off to a higher stage. I am making ?1,00,000 from my side business and I absolutely love every part of it. I am indeed happy that it offers me a healthy culture, a positive working atmosphere and fuels my confidence."

Ensure that you write your affirmations 3, 6 and 9 times in your morning, day and night. It shouldn't be any less or more than these prescribed numbers. The point is to trick your mind into believing that you already have these wishes turned into a reality, and the Universe collaborates from there.

Using manifesting is an excellent way to recalibrate the energy you're putting into the Universe. Try to welcome affirmative changes that the Universe sends your way and catch them before it slips away from you. It's in your hands to make this process a lot easier for the Universe by co-creating with it.

For example, if you want the man or woman of your dream who is understanding, emotionally available and reliable, start showing up that way first. Make sure you up your social game, introduce yourself to people and do the self-growth work.

And, if you are rooting for better financial prospects, start looking out for new jobs–part-time, freelance, or any partnership opportunities that come your way. Get yourself into investing, or take assistance from a financial advisor. Let your intuition guide you as you prepare your life for all the good energy you're calling in!

Now, the second technique–the 55x5 method.

Theory behind 55x5:

55x5 technique is basically a mixture of two law of attraction tools–affirmations and journaling, pretty much like the 369 one. The only difference is the time.

While the 369 technique needs to be carried out for 33 days, the 55x5 one needs to be carried out for only five days, but then 55 times a day compared to 3,6 and 9 in the former.

The similarity being, both work on the principles of repeating positively formulated statements which eventually play an effect on your subconscious mind and signal the Universe to co-create it with you.

Repeatedly writing a positive affirmation allows you to draw in a vibrational match for what you want in your life.

Now, the steps:

Step 1: Choose what you want to manifest. This is where you need to be crystal clear about what you want.

And,

Step 2: Write your affirmation 55 times for five days.

You might think that 55 times is a lot more compared to 3+6+9 = 18 times a day (which is almost thrice), but remember, the higher the written affirmations, the quicker you raise your energetic vibrations. This makes you more vibrationally aligned with your desire.

When you write 55 times, you're 55 times more in sync with what you first started. To get the most out of the 55×5 technique is to not only write your affirmation but to truly feel it.

Let the positive message raise your energy. Soak in the high vibrational energies of your body, mind, and spirit. Trust that the work you've put in over the past five days will attract your desires to you. When you feel good from within, you become a magnet for miracles.

Let's hop on to the third technique–the Pillow technique.

Theory behind the Pillow technique:

Even though you might presume that you slip into a different world of inactivity and inertness when you sleep, that's where you could go wrong. Your thoughts and subconsciousness are still pretty active.

The time before you fall asleep to when you're completely awoken is the theta phase. During this phase, your subconscious mind is most susceptible to wire your intentions, thoughts and wishes.

Succinctly put, your last thoughts of the day positively impact your dream state, which carries through to your following day. If you're new to the manifestation process, this technique comes in handy and is beginner-friendly.

Steps:

Step 1: Onboard more clarity on what you want to manifest. Have a razor-sharp focus on the specifics of your wish.

Step 2: Take a sheet out of your journal or grab a paper and write your wish down. Follow the practices you've learned early in this book: present-tensed, positive and to-the-point sentences work best. For example, if you're manifesting better health, you could write something like:

"I have a healthy and a strong body. I am healing my body with positive thoughts, actions and energy. I am able to take good care of my health. I feel healthy from within."

Step 3: Now comes the most important step. The whole point of this technique is to have your manifestations the last thought on your mind before you sleep. Read out your wish from the paper and repeat saying it as many times as you'd like. Since you wrote it as if you already have it, it will produce a feel-good emotion. Now, put this piece of paper underneath your pillow.

Step 4: Visualise and think about those sentences that you just read. Imagine that it has come true and you're already living it.

Step 5: Sleep.

There aren't any specific timelines as to how long you should be doing this. If done right, you should be able to see your desired results real quick. Follow along with this process until your wishes come true.

Now, the fourth and the final technique—the Two Cup technique.

Theory behind the Two Cup Technique:

Manifesting your desires just got as simple as drinking a cup of water. This technique combines visualisation and a concept called "dimension jumping". As the name denotes, it is based on the idea that multiple dimensions or realities can exist on the same timeline and that we can jump and shift to any of these realities. These are the steps:

Step 1: Take two cups. Fill one with water and leave the other one empty.

Step 2: Write your affirmations on a post-it note and stick it onto the water-filled cup stating your current reality. Similarly, write your desired affirmations on a post-it note and stick it to the empty cup.

For example, you could write something like:

Cup 1: *"I am not living in a grand, beautiful apartment."*

Cup 2: *"I am grateful to live in my dream home."* or *"My new apartment is waiting for me, I can feel it."*

Step 3: Think about your current reality and ponder how you'd like your current reality to elevate. Focus on the positive feelings of your desired reality and pour the water from the current cup into the second cup. While pouring it, concentrate on the joyful feelings of newness, gratitude and positivity.

Step 4: By focusing on the written affirmations, drink the water and know that you're now perfectly aligned with the vibrations you're manifesting in your reality.

DIY Exercise

This is where you pick one of your favourite techniques and perform it. Make sure you stick to the steps prescribed in the chapter. Commit yourself to the process and believe in the power of scripting. It has worked out for me and many who believe in the power of the law of attraction.

P.S: Consistency goes a long way. Scripting is all about offering a chance to explore your desires intricately. When you script, you're naturally drawn a step closer to your manifestations. However, to make the best out of it, peruse a couple of guidelines to help you manifest better. This is what the next chapter holds for us.

CHAPTER TEN

GOVERNING GUIDELINES

While some might claim manifesting is daunting, others say it is no rocket science. Truth be told, it's neither!

What matters is what you believe in. Know that your dreams will come true sooner than later. But for that to happen, there are some first-things-first you should abide by to slip into a manifestation grip:

Guideline #1: Remember to feel it through

You aren't maintaining a journal just for the sake of writing. You want to engage at a deeper surface of your imaginative skills and let your desires form a clear picture in your head. That's why you need to feel your manifestation like you mean it!

For example, if you're thinking of a new house, start visualising yourself getting into a brand-new apartment with every amenity you once wished for. The trick here is to place yourself inside this house and let yourself feel that you're in it.

The techniques prescribed in Chapter 9 tell us how to get started with the manifestation exercises. Now, you may be able to write your affirmations a zillion times, but the whole point of it turning them into a reality seizes when you don't feel it from within.

The more you trust the process, the Universe, too, will bless back with a trusting reward. All you need to do is embrace the change and feel your intentions.

Guideline #2: Speak it out

Without a doubt, writing is powerful. Now, if you could club it with speaking, you start accentuating your manifestation. If you're uncomfortable speaking your private wishes to someone else, you can speak it out to yourself in an empty room.

Speak for an ideal time–a minute, 10 minutes, or an hour–your call! Be it writing or speaking, have faith that you have the power to create your reality by speaking it into being.

Words that you speak are energy, just like everything else around you. And you're already aware of the magnanimous power energy has to match your desired wishes toward you.

Dedicate your words with conviction and true feelings and the Universe will hear you. Talk to the Universe and ask:

"How can I find a little extra strength?"

"Am I on the right path?"

"Do I need a gentle nudge to go in the right direction?"

Don't lock feelings inside you–that's not healthy.

Instead, talk to the Universe like a friend and tell it what you desire. It won't be long before you sense a response back from Universe through signs, symbols, and loving messages.

Guideline #3: Break it into bite-sized steps

Let's assume you want to be an actor and that's what you're manifesting with this book's help. To be an actor, you need a few prerequisites. Top of the list is acting skills, perfect dialogue delivery, enunciated diction, ability to understand emotions, patience to take re-takes and many more.

The trick is to break these bits into smaller sections. This simple yet overlooked aspect marks a profound difference in receiving desired manifestations.

Each day, you take a small step closer to your dreams. You might start by watching your favourite actors and learning their methods. Or, taking up an acting class too. If you fumble or have a habit of incoherent speech, perhaps now is when you can take the first step toward honing your diction to perfection.

Grab the opportunity to take bite-sized steps toward your dreams. This small step could be anything, as long as it comes from a place that feels good and right to you.

I know, small steps don't seem so cool, especially when you're strapped for time and want your dreams to be fulfilled this very second. But, let me put it this way: a small step a day for the next seven days gives you seven steps ahead of where you're now.

Guideline #4: Have fun

The whole point of this book is to make you feel good about what you are doing. I don't want you to work out the DIY exercises from this book as if it were a math problem! Relish the process and trust the Universe; you'll see a positive difference.

Stay true to your personal style. Express gratitude for what comes your way.

And make sure you have fun–because that's what matters.

That being said, start finding happiness with the little things in life. Remember, it starts small but expands hugely.

Believe in the process and, most importantly, believe in yourself.

"You are living your dreams."

"You can make it happen."

"You have got this."

P.S: Now, you have all it takes to swim into the flow of manifestation. This can only happen when you truly connect to your soul. Understand and know what you want from life. Remove every speck of limiting beliefs that fall in your way. You don't deserve them.

It's time to learn how to weave your thoughts and knowledge learnt so far and wreathe them into a more assertive approach.

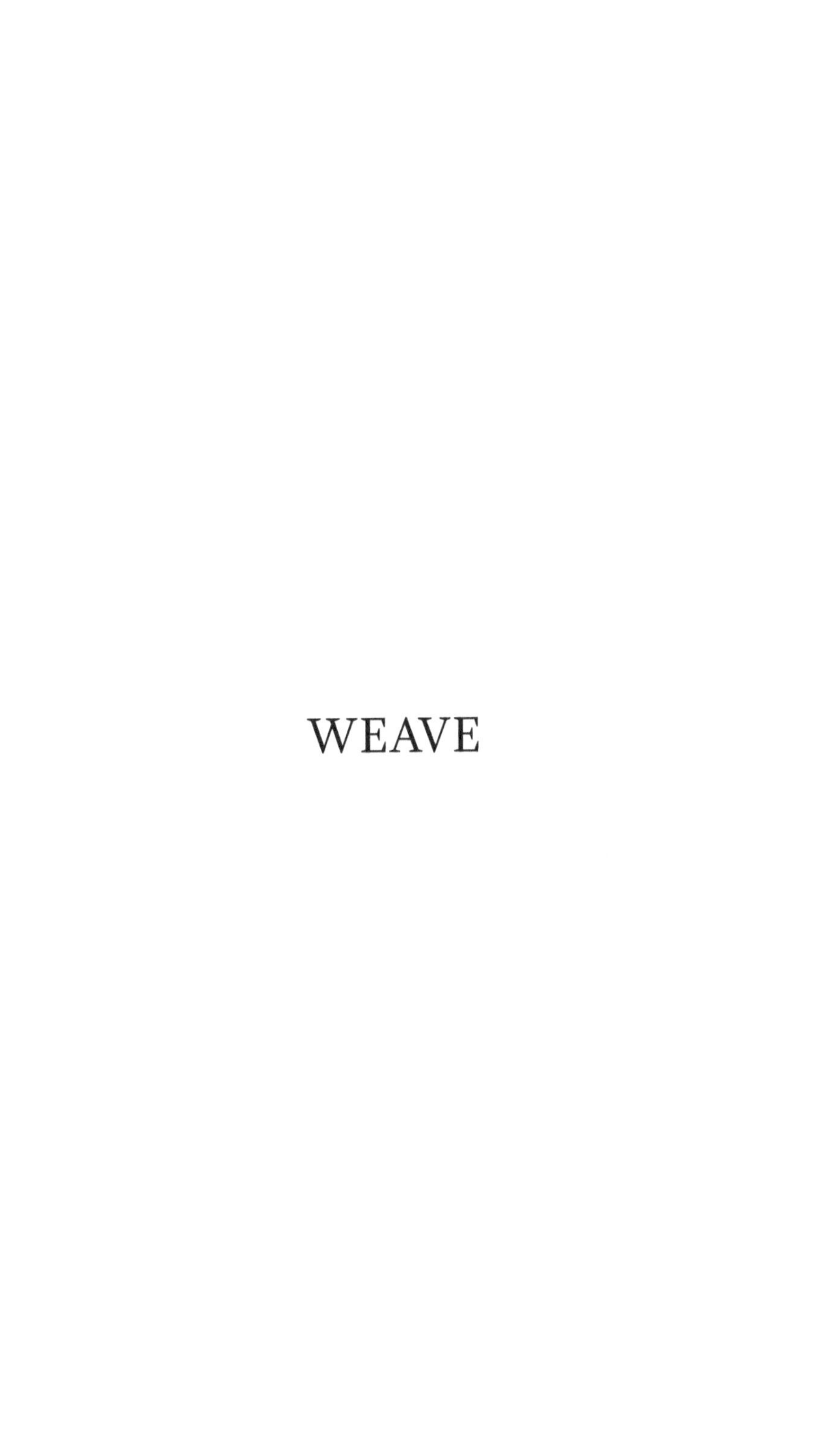

WEAVE

CHAPTER ELEVEN

BALANCING THE KOKORO

To lead a happy life, striking the right balance is quintessential. The chapters thus far have taught you the virtues of affirmations, positivity and gratitude. It's time to tap into the biggest virtue that must reside within ourselves: balance.

From our professional spheres, eating habits, lifestyle to personal relationships, we ought to strike a perfect balance. This starts with you and is best described in the Japanese concept, *Kokoro*. This elaborates that the alignment of the mind, body and soul are linked and can't be inseparable from one another.

Before diving any further into how to create a healthy balance between your mind, body and soul, we'll take a step back to understand a Chinese philosophy involving *yang* and *yin* energy.

Yang is Chinese for males and represents masculinity, activity and light.

Yin is Chinese for females and represents femininity, passivity and darkness.

This Chinese philosophy describes that these opposing forces should be interdependent and interconnected in our real world to weave a perfect balance. (That's what Part III of this book is all about.)

While *yang* energy reflects upon your assertive facets, characterised by vigour, exteriority, hardness or dryness, *yin* energy, on the contrary, is known for its non-assertive aspects like interiority, softness or dewiness.

The *yin-yang* energies are constantly influencing each other. Both aspects should be in sync to dwell in dynamic equilibrium. When one characteristic tends to tone down, the other should pep up to balance it.

If you like to dictate things and want them to work out your way, or if you're less emotional and wish to see yourself as the final decision-maker, your *yang* energy supersedes your *yin* energy. To have parity in life, charge up your *yin* side. And remember, this can be the case for both men and women.

In the sacred unity of *Kokoro*, your mind is associated with *yang* energy. It's the centre of all your thoughts. Your thoughts today turn into a plausible dream tomorrow. Viewing your life from a balanced perspective will help you make the right choices.

Similarly, your soul is associated with *yin* energy. If you want to abide by set rules, are very emotional when it comes to a difficult situation or want someone else to make the final decisions, your *yin* energy is superior to your *yang* energy.

And finally, the body is said to be the reflection of the *yang* and *yin* energies, namely your mind and soul. The body is essentially the place where your mind and soul meet.

A stable mind and a clear soul give rise to a healthy body. How you deal with this polarity is what gets reflected in you. Therefore, pay special attention to your body and don't take it lightly. Nourish your body with healthy diets, physical exercise, and loads of positive thoughts.

Introspect the *yang* and *yin* aspects that reside within you. Learn where you lack and re-tune your actions accordingly. Take this up as a lesson to evaluate yourself.

The ability to love yourself precedes the ability to love others.

Don't go too hard on yourself; compliment yourself when you achieve something–no matter how small the achievement is. Appreciate your efforts. Unearth and dig deeper into the special qualities that make you feel unique.

You'll feel the difference, and this will make you love yourself.

You only live once—make the most out of your life.

DIY Exercise

This time around, I won't be asking you to take out your journal. Instead, I want you to *do* this do-it-yourself exercise. So, what do you need to do?

It's time for you to take a break from everything. You might have had a really long day where you sat through endless meetings, experimented in your lab or attended the six-hour workshop. Think of an activity that will refresh your *Kokoro*.

Think of something that revitalises your mind.

It could be listening to a peaceful, calming song. If you spent your whole day on your phone or laptop, this is a great time to break free and give yourself a digital detox.

Now, think of something that revitalises your body.

Go out for brisk jogging. Walk your dog. Else, stretch out in your room. That helps, too. Treat yourself to some salon-style pedicure or facial. If you don't want to do any of these, simply take a nap. Yes! Never underestimate the power of good sleep.

And finally, think of something that revitalises your soul.

This is the best part. Here's what you do to feed your soul. Do something you always wish you had time for but never managed to do. You should honestly look forward to this. And it can be anything.

P.S: If music soothes your soul, have at it. If food is what tops the list, raid your fridge or order something nice. Get into the habit of treating yourself well and loving yourself no matter what. This brings us to our next chapter when we learn more about the subtle art of practising habits.

CHAPTER TWELVE

PRACTISING HABITS

The very basics of achieving something in life start with a habit.

It might propel a few pre-conditioned efforts to fall in the flow, but once you get the hang of it, it becomes a part of your life. Then, you no longer have to remind yourself to follow them consciously. Forming the right habit is of great interest to most of us, mainly due to its power to discipline us.

That's because habits are the ultimate form of self-improvement. It is what builds our life. They can specifically augment the quality of your life; soon, you'll realise that its effects are multiplying.

Your day starts with your habits. Doesn't it?

What is the first thing you do when you wake up in the morning? Hitting the gym? Making a quick breakfast? Updating yourself with the latest news? Or simply meditating?

The beauty of practising habits daily lies in its simplicity.

You pick something small and then expand on it. It's the art of managing your time–effectively and logically.

Split your 24 hours a day evenly. Allot some hours for your job, some for your family and reserve some only for yourself. This could include taking time out to read your favourite novel, getting a massage, shopping, or simply pampering yourself with some binge-watch time.

In fact, there is nothing wrong with binge-watching OTT platforms every day. If anything, it gives you the liberty to form a habit. How?

Now, you have a prescribed number of hours to watch your favourite shows, doing something you like while habituating it.

Every day presents you with a fresh opportunity to try something new, experience happiness and create abundance. After all, the basics of the law of attraction teach you that. You see, the law of attraction is not really about begging for your dream life from the Universe; it's all about attracting it toward you.

All you need to do is to use these habits to build new practices that help manifest your dream life.

For example, if you're into playback singing and wish to make a career out of it, make it a point to practise hitting the right notes or doing a vocal workout. Better yet, hire a professional to help you. Adding this to your routine will help you stay focused and perform better. You might as well add them before or after your already existing habits.

For instance,

"I will practice singing after I return from the gym."

Setting up your manifestation goals as a habit in your routine will ensure that you don't skip on them and get more done in a limited time. And when you successfully follow a routine, this will give you happiness and satisfaction because *"you did it."*

You will start to feel good about yourselves, which is our ultimate goal, right? Now, you get to set some time off for your work and do something that fuels your big dream.

Feeling good about what you do is important. Don't forget to give yourself a pat on the back whenever this happens.

If it helps, start spending time with Mother Nature. Even though it sounds lunatic, you'll feel a difference. Nature has the power to uplift our emotions.

So, when you go back to work on your big dream, you'll be more inspired to do so. That is mainly because self-care aids in decluttering your head and giving you mental clarity.

Adding a daily habit to your routine will discipline your life and help you commit to the process. Sooner than later, you'll start to love this change.

When you direct your day by feeding it with the goals that your dream entails, you're in a better place already. Even when you find hindrances that come along your route for maintaining these habits, that won't be an issue anymore as now you know how to take care of yourself.

DIY Exercise

Pick five habits that are a must to follow your dreams.

For example, you want to represent your country in sports, say, Javelin throw. To accomplish that, you need to set some stringent daily habits. It could be something like:

1. Practising the skill-set needed for this sport–the drills, flexibility, speed, or maybe the nuances.

2. Hiring a coach.

3. Maintaining a balanced diet or staying fit.

4. Understanding the sport through technical aspects.

5. Determination to win.

Similarly, your list can go on. But, first, I want you to think of those habits that will bring out the best in you. What makes you happy? Use the space here to mention five such daily habits which, when followed, will help you commit to the process.

1.

2.

3.

4.

5.

P.S: Scientifically proven, it's said that we need only 21 days to form a habit. If you stick with a particular habit for just 21 days, this already becomes a part of your routine–know it or not.

A little habit you form today will spark a significant difference in your tomorrow. The intensity that picks up from these habits will amaze you. There is a high chance that you'll stick to it from now on, as you're habituated to it. And once you're habituated, you'll find this intensity getting bigger and better, making it possible for you to manifest quicker.

CHAPTER THIRTEEN

Understanding Meditation

To truly get to your inner self, you must have a fundamental understanding of meditation. The art of meditating is all about nailing your focus onto a specific subject while tuning out everything around you. The sooner you know of its power, the easier it becomes to connect with your true soul.

Meditating for as little as ten minutes daily can unravel your thought process and filter only positive thinking.

Let's look at it this way: how great does your laptop perform when you have a hundred tabs on? To top that, it starts to warm up incessantly due to the excessive heat. It hangs unreasonably and this pauses your work, which is irksome. What do you do in a situation like that? If it were me, I would immediately reset or restart it.

The same works with our lives too.

When we deal with our life and its troubles, our mind catches this chaos and frustrates us. Meditation is *that* reset button that allows you to start again from a peaceful mode.

Meditation is something that a lot of people misunderstand. This chapter aims to break through such notions and help you understand its essence as seamlessly as possible.

Decluttering your mind is crucial to lead a happy life. And meditation is the ultimate mind-clearer.

When you gain more freedom of thought in any situation, you'll begin to feel your true power.

Think of these questions:

"How can I stay put and collected even when I am under stress?"

"What do I do when I get these negative emotional triggers in my mind?"

"Is it even possible to not think about anything at any given point in time?"

With meditation, these answers will surface within you. It gives you the ability to pause in the middle of your thought process and say: *"Is this really my choice? If I could choose, is this what I would want to think?"*

Now, let's put this into perspective.

People think of meditation as a severe cerebral exercise. It's not. It's all about learning to focus. That's all!

Converge your attention onto your dream for a set amount of time. And let's say you can't fix right into focusing on a single subject in the beginning; let me assure you– that's completely normal. After all, *"Practice makes a man perfect."*

~~~~~

DIY Exercise

Understanding meditation doesn't need to be overwhelming. Here are a few tips for beginning with:

- **Select a specific time of the day when you're distraction-free**
~~~~~

Meditations work best during the morning hours, but if you're too busy, pick anytime during the rest of your day. Ensure that this time is yours and non-negotiable.

Some might start planning a meditation session for 30 minutes a day, but I suggest you begin with 10 minutes. Slowly, you can time yourself to 15, then 20 and eventually 30. However, refrain from timing yourself for 30 minutes on the first day of meditation. Like I've mentioned earlier, go easy on yourself.

- **Prefer a consistent place**

Find a place in and around you that has the slightest disturbance. The quieter you've around you, the easier it is to practice meditation.

Also, steer away from your mobile phone, tabs, and laptops for this duration. Think of these 10 minutes as your "me-time." If it helps, you can turn on some yoga music. Music has the power to calm your nervous system and regulate your practice with harmony.

- **Settle in with ease**

Get comfy with a position. If being seated in a chair is what makes you comfortable, so be it. If sitting out on the floor with a mat is your pick, that works too. However, refrain from lying down for this exercise. There is a good chance that you might doze off! Ideally, the best position is to cross your legs in a sitting position and let your hands rest on your knees, with your palms facing up.

- **Relax, inhale and exhale**

Close your eyes and loosen your body. Study the pattern of your breathing.

Let me introduce a breathing technique to you: the box breathing technique. This is also said to be the 4 4 4 4 method.

As the name suggests, this technique asks you to take 4 seconds to breathe in, 4 seconds to hold this air in your lungs, 4 seconds to exhale and 4 seconds to keep your lungs empty. Focus on pacing it right. And observe how this slowly takes you into a state of calmness and bliss.

- **Make it a habit**

As we discussed in our earlier chapter, practising a habit daily habit is what we need to imbibe discipline in our lives. Ensure that you make it a point to meditate every day at your given time and place. Start small; trust me, you'll enjoy every bit of this process.

P.S: Once you have completed your session, don't forget to give yourself a little treat. Check your social media, draw a warm bath, or visit your favourite bakery—whichever works.

This reward will make you want to keep doing meditation every day. Bonus points if you check in with yourself to see how you feel doing that reward. If it's something you already do, you might start to feel slightly different, or you might start to become more aware of how you feel when you do it.

CHAPTER FOURTEEN

THE PLACEBO EFFECT

The connection between mind and body is happening inside you, feel it or not. Just like the law of attraction, there goes another scientifically-proven phenomenon that can unlock the mind-body connection, namely the Placebo Effect.

So, what is the Placebo Effect?

The placebo effect decodes and demonstrates the powerfully undeniable connection between the mind and body, the way we feel. The more you think of a certain outcome, the higher the probability you'll experience it.

And the same works for adverse outcomes as well. The more you question your capabilities and expect negative results on your door, the better the chances they'll turn true.

As they say, *"Be careful what you wish for."* Circling back to the very essence of this chapter, weaving positive thoughts will wreathe into positive outcomes and weaving negative thoughts will wreathe into negative outcomes.

Let me break it into a bite-sized real-life example:

You have a severe headache and your body is going into reboot mode. Your doctor gives you a pill and assures you that this should work within 30 minutes and you'll be out of the bad headache. It's 30 minutes now and you start feeling the exact words that your doctor just said.

How did that happen?

That's the placebo effect.

The doctor's assurance that you'll feel better within 30 minutes signalled your mind that your body is recuperating. Technically, this prescribed pill had nothing to do with your headache. It was solely your belief that the doctor's word and the pill would make you feel better, and that's that.

You'd have faced different versions of placebos in your day-to-day life. When someone says you look 2X more attractive when you bring on your prettiest smile, this instantly makes you smile. And now you're smiling, aren't you?

Through the lens of research, placebos are generally used by medical practitioners or researchers to discern the effects of a tablet or a drug. Science states that sometimes putting a patient under a placebo can give away just as effective results as an actual medical treatment.

This simply means placebos kindle your imagination to convince the body that it's easing and you're starting to heal, almost magically. That's because the very thought in your mind induces you to believe that these prescribed pills are taking your illness away, leaving you with an actual, beneficial response.

It is speculated that a driving force behind the success of placebos is the ritual itself, the simple act of taking a pill as though it is the medicine that stimulates the results in the body. The positive perception of treatment may stimulate the brain to think the body is being healed.

How does this work?

Our emotions fuel our thought processes.

Our thoughts charge up when we add emotions to them, making them come alive. This furthers the message to our brain to transform the process of converting thoughts into a tangible manifestation.

Your brain produces certain chemicals that make you feel what you think. When you think of happy thoughts, you suddenly feel this sudden urge of happiness, giving you a feel-good moment.

Similarly, when you think of a time when you feel lost, desolated, or unhappy, you start getting this cringe-worthy feeling, which isn't pleasant.

Your thought process is an integral part of manifestation. You might say that there float tens of thousands of thoughts in your head about your dream life that you choose to manifest, but something or the other isn't working out. Yes, it won't unless you give it a kick.

Start with placing a dedicated feeling behind your dream, followed by a stern belief that you want this to turn true, followed by conscious awareness that you'll make it happen. That's what Part III of this book teaches you, to weave thoughtful actions governed by a trusting belief to manifest your dreams.

The efficacy of placebo effects and the law of attraction demonstrates that we always have control over our fate and reality to some extent!

A well-defined mind-body connection will enable you to draw more of what you want and less of what you don't. Know that it's very much doable to manifest a healthy mind and body, relationships and life. All you need is the guiding tools and, most of all, conviction. Your brain is limitless and you can shift to your desired reality.

DIY Exercise

It's time to get you to a quick do-it-yourself exercise to understand the mind-body connection. Again, this is one such exercise where I won't ask you to pull out your journal. This is going to be solely a mind-body exercise.

1. Ask your mind and body what you want in your life? Figure out what you wish to manifest and why. While your mind will give you the mental strength to fuel your dreams, your body will physically make it possible.

Let's say you face extreme hair fall and no medication, exercise or hacks work out for you. I know this can sound ridiculously trivial, but it happens to many people, especially women, and consciously or unconsciously, it starts hampering your confidence. (Well, it did mine.) Now, you want a way out of that and prepare yourself mentally and physically to make your placebo turn into a reality.

2. Next, consider some healthy habits you could use as your placebo. It could be something like brushing your hair regularly, making it tangle-free, silkier and easier to manage.

Determine why you're getting a massive amount of hair fall. Is it because of some vitamin deficiency? Bad weather? Or due to stress and a sedentary lifestyle? Some of you might not be able to relate to this example entirely, but it doesn't have to make sense as long as you understand the concept.

3. Now, try to do your placebo and start imbibing the process that you're getting thick, luscious hair back again. You're no longer under the clutches of severe hair loss and

are improving day by day.

P.S: You can take up any other mind-body exercise that works for you. What you think is what you manifest. You'll slowly see that the right combination of mind-body connections will make it happen. Remember to stay positive; that will help you reach your goal easily!

CHAPTER FIFTEEN

ALIGNING ACTIONS

The Universe cares about your thoughts and beliefs and pays conscious attention to the actions that evolve from your intentions. When you want something with your heart and soul, prove to the Universe that you're taking all the right steps and it will reap you the desired rewards.

You might have heard people say, *"I have a good feeling about this," "I think my soulmate is around the corner,"* or *"I've been feeling my dream job is going to knock on my door."* While it sure can, this doesn't necessarily mean you have to sit back and watch things happen on their own.

For starters, what actions are you taking if you want to meet the man or woman of your dreams? Are you socializing with peers? Are you upping your date game?

And if you're under the impression that a Fortune 100 company will ring you and offer you a great role with greater pay, how would that magically spin? Have you updated your resume? Are you applying to your dream companies? Are you honing your skill set with the specific certifications and degrees your job demands?

This might compel you to think, *"I do everything I can, within my limits, but it still doesn't pan out,"* *"Nothing good ever happens to me,"* *"God hates me,"* or *"I'm unlucky."*

You could have probably thought of such statements more than once, and that's completely normal and, if anything, pretty natural! Of course, destiny is one thing, but then it's not like we've no control over it. We sure do!

This is your life and you have the gears. Empowering yourself begins with owning responsibility of everything that happens in your life.

That means you need to take inspired action to manifest what you want, big or small. As mentioned above, your energy always attracts experiences that match your vibration.

Think of a magnet.

I'm sure you would have played with a piece of magnet before. Have you been astonished by its ability to attract iron elements as if it were happening magically? Upon close observation, you'll realise that the magnet attracts iron only when you bring it closer. Getting the magnet closer to the iron is the action you had to take to see the magic.

The same trick applies to attracting your desires and wishes. Infusing your actions with positive energy cultivated in your manifestation practices can channel it toward your dream.

There is no secret formula when it comes to taking action.

The only thing that matters here is *taking* action. Start small if you're unsure what and how to do things. Then expand on it. Starting with something will allow you to see the bigger picture and give you the confidence to make things bigger and better.

And trust me, this is a lot better than not doing anything because you're scared, overwhelmed, or aimless.

You may wonder, aren't affirmations, manifestation tools, visualisations, or vision boards not enough to get the needle moving? As much as I hate to break it to you, they aren't! Unless you don't fuel them with inspired action, things won't go out as planned. Dare to take action that aligns with your dreams.

DIY Exercise

Time to pull out your journal for yet another exciting exercise!

Think of an intention, part of what you wish to manifest. Now, write five action steps that you can take toward it. Here's an example:

Let's assume that your intention here is to become a writer. You want to see yourself in a rewarding position in the writing industry and that's what you'd like to manifest.

Next, your action steps for today could be looking out for available writing positions online on LinkedIn. You could take a writing course or ask your connections if there is an opening at their company. I manifested becoming a published author and this is my first book already. And I couldn't be more proud.

So, grab that pen and start fuelling your intentions with the right course of action. Use this space to go creative with your ideas.

1.

2.

3.

4.

5.

P.S: Things don't happen on their own; you make them happen. Identify them and let them shine through you!

71

WELCOME

CHAPTER SIXTEEN

LOOSENING LIMITATIONS

The last chapter taught us that taking action is what brings us a step closer to dreams. But, a part of these actions is to let go of the limitations in your way.

What are these limitations? Another fancy term in the dictionary of manifestations? Well, let's look at this example to answer it.

Do you ever think this way?

"I don't have what it takes,"

"I can't do this,"

"I might not succeed,"

"It's extremely tough,"

If you hop on these thoughts more than a couple of times a day, that's okay! These are the limitations you need to sweep off.

There is nothing wrong with hitting a multitude of roadblocks or rock bottom when something doesn't go as planned, especially when you really wanted it. Don't be afraid of what's coming your way. Instead, welcome it!

What if you tackle it and find yourself in a new zone filled with joy, abundance, happiness, growth and success?

But if you don't have the drive to deal with it, you might as well be losing out on these.

Think of it as an opportunity in disguise to re-address and realign with your actions. That way, you realise you're out of alignment and gift yourself a chance to readjust.

Allow the space and time to surface what's bubbling underneath to reveal itself. With that, you'll find a great lesson that teaches you to stop repenting.

Carving a bigger room for positive affirmations lets you see what you're missing from life. The more you dig into limitations that hinder your dream, you give them a chance to prosper which is precisely what you need to refrain from.

Derail from this place of self-doubt. You can experience the life of your dreams only when you're completely secure with yourself. Accept these limitations as they come and allow yourself to let go of them. Think of these limits as an open opportunity. Behind every limit lies a wonderful chance to explore.

Sometimes we wrap ourselves in this cocoon of limits that we can reach only a certain amount of happiness, prosperity, money or growth in our lives. We draw this limiting perimeter around us that we aren't supposed to surpass.

Do you think of such questions?

"If I already have my dream house, how can I also have my dream car?

"How can I be physically fit if I'm already financially sound?"

Something has to go amiss, right?

Questioning whether you can have the best of both worlds is basically limiting your beliefs. Yes, you can bear multiple successful traits and still joggle them smoothly without letting the ball drop once. Allow them to surface, note your limiting beliefs and let them go.

Shape your perspective. Every time you take a step forward; it's possible to see blockages. But this only means that you're progressing ahead. So, great work there!

Know that your manifestations are on the way. Have faith in the Universe. Believe in the fact that the scale is tipping in your favour. Once you do, you can feel good about resistance. End the cycle of self-restraint and open up to the possibility of even greater happiness.

The biggest blockage that stops you from getting what you want is when you consistently focus on the lack of it. The more you look at the limitations, the more you let the Universe know that you don't have them. When you don't let go of these limitations, you get in the way of the Universe delivering what you want.

DIY Exercise

This exercise will help you deal with your urge to change the current circumstance of your life. By accepting the circumstance you're in, you're not giving in or telling the Universe that you don't care about it being fixed. By letting go of your need to fix it right now, you let the Universe do what it needs to do to get you what you want.

Write five statements that currently bother you in your life and mention the phrase *"It's okay that"* before that.

For example:

"It's okay that I'm feeling grumpy and I'm not sure why."

"It's okay that I couldn't win the first prize in yesterday's competition."

"It's okay that I haven't made enough profits from the stock market today."

Use the space below to fill in with your top five.

1.

2.

3.

4.

5.

P.S: We all have something in our life that others could be manifesting to have at the moment. You just don't know it yet. The Universe wants to take care of you. This exercise is to feel relief. When you account for your limiting beliefs, you make peace with them.

CHAPTER SEVENTEEN

ACCEPTING CHANGES

What's crucial is to accept the changes that follow up from these loosened limitations. You've begun manifesting your truest desires. It's now time to take a step closer and prepare yourself to adapt to the changes that come your way.

You might get terrified of what these changes might look like. You could also be apprehensive about making room for the new changes, which is fine!

The power to sail through life from the current stance to the future of your dreams lies in your hand. You design your life. It's about how well you tune into the right frequencies to experience it. For that, you need to let go of your fear.

The fear of change.

Any change will trigger a warning in your head before you implement it, even a positive one. You'll have dozens of questions in and around it.

"Should I apply for this job? What if I am not qualified enough and get rejected?"

"Could I ever win the contest? What if I am eliminated?"

"Would my boss accept my request for a salary hike? What if she discards it?"

While you're on these questions, thoughts like the following might break into your mind:

"Changes will adversely affect me."

"I'd stop changes from happening in any way I can."

"I resist changes."

It is human nature to apprehend the presence of a change happening with and around you. Unless you don't sense things panning out the way you planned, you let yourself believe it's not for you or it'll never happen. Pressing forward and staying on the course despite these trails of thoughts is what you need to battle through.

For example, you're new to swimming.

Your coach suggests you try an approach as a beginner. You're sold out with its impact the first time. But when you try, later on, you never seem to get that same intensity of joy any time after. That's when you assume that the approach has lost its charm.

On the contrary, what happened is that your mind and body acclimated to your new state of belief, *"It's not for me." I don't think I can ever swim," 'I'd rather drown."*

But, there wasn't anything wrong with the approach. You felt it was right, yet you didn't act on it. Had you still given it a chance and practised more to execute it, it would still work exactly as it should have without you realising it.

Have you heard the adage, *"Be the change you want to see in the world?"*

Simply put, start small and start with yourself.

Your physical space reflects upon your mental space. Meaning, that if your surroundings are unkempt, this inadvertently affects your frame of mind too.

Have you noticed how entering a well-lit, sweet-fragrant room instantly uplifts your mood?

From a logical perspective, you automatically feel at ease and relaxed when you see things around you placed in a particular order. Now compare this to walking into a room with pretty much the opposite and watch how instantly that turns you off.

Look around in your room. Is everything where it needs to be? Start with clearing out your desk. Throw out the junk in your kitchen that you no longer need. Declutter that old cupboard. Fresh, lovely flowers on your table won't hurt.

The more you hide your dirty clutter, the more it hinders your aura and prevents the positive flow of energy from getting to you. When we shun away from our present, we automatically stop moving toward our future.

A cleansed aura has the power to elevate our physical, mental, spiritual and emotional space. That'll take you into a high-vibrational mode. With this, you're allowing newness to accommodate–a change that'll make you chase your dream.

DIY Exercise

Take time off from whatever you're doing and change your surrounding space.

For starters, are there heaps of laundry you're yet to attend to? Now is the time.

Do you have a favourite drawer where you tuck your whole world inside? Let's get rid of that.

Does your bed have a hidden compartment where you stash unmentionable stuff? I guess you need to attend to it as well.

P.S: Even though these tiny bits of clutter might seem negligible, they play a vital role in disrupting the positive flow of energy.

Being organisational does more good than you'd wonder. Changing your physical space from the mundane old lot to something warm, welcoming and beckoning will boost your energy and make you feel good. Start small, be prepared to accept changes and you'll find happiness.

CHAPTER EIGHTEEN

NEGATING NEGATIVITY

Let's face it, adapting to changes with the hope that it'll indeed work out in your favour is a scary thought. What's more bewildering is that you might face times when you question the essence of manifestations if you don't see the results real quick.

Which is fine, to be honest.

But once these wandering thoughts enter your mind, don't let them transform into negativity. Recognize you're having a negative moment but then strive to spin it into a positive one.

It's easy to see the negative side of things.

When you see yourself slipping into a quicksand of negative thoughts, pivot yourself back to the positive ones.

Know that obstacles are inevitable. When you see through them, you'll find a hidden opportunity in disguise to tap on.

Steering away from negative thoughts isn't practical at all times. However, the more you think about the things you don't have in your life, you add to the negativity quotient.

Instead, focus on what you already have. That way, it makes it easier to drift away from negative thoughts.

Also, don't be scared of the word "no." There is nothing wrong with saying no. I would say saying "no" is a subtle art. With "no," you're demarcating clear boundaries with the Universe. Every time you see a situation where you're tempted to say "yes" while you know saying "no" is the right thing to do, affirm the following:

"No. Thank you. I trust a bigger, better version will come my way, which is more in sync with my dream."

See what you did here?

By denying things you don't feel good about, you're letting more room for what you're worthy of. Don't let your guards down and don't settle for something that you deserve more of. Know that you're worthy and deserving, something we'll read more about in Chapter 24 of this book.

You could debate how I can stay away from negative thoughts when my wishes aren't fulfilled and my dreams are not even close to where I see them.

It starts with seeing the silver lining of a cloud. You need to trace the positivity even when you find a negative situation.

How do I do that?

Staying away from negativity starts with distancing from people who add negative thoughts to your head. You might stumble on people who love complaining or gossiping.

You may think, *"I really don't have control over what others talk about," "I can't do anything about it," and "I'm not responsible."*

That's untrue.

Instead, use your time with the right people who boost your mood and energy. Show it to the Universe that you love being in a space where you are loved, respected and where you can resonate with high-vibrational energies. When you meet someone who is positively energetic, happy and fun, try to match up to their vibration by pepping yours up.

DIY Exercise

Mention a thought that you'd like to reframe. It can be any wandering negative thoughts that run through your mind. For example, you could be currently feeling something like:

"I'm not determined enough."

"I can't do this task right."

"I will have to deal with this situation."

Instead, try to reframe these statements as:

"I'm ready to be determined."

"I'm grateful to find this task."

"I'm happy that I get to see this opportunity."

You'll start to feel the difference just by reframing your statements.

P.S: Staying away from negativity starts by surrounding yourself with positive people. For this, get outside your comfort zone and look for a group to meet and interact with like-minded people. Alternatively, you can join an online session with a professional coach who can help you battle negativity with positivity.

FACING FEARS

What's stopping you from accepting changes? What holds you back from your next steps? Is it the uncertainty of failure and rejection? Societal pressure? Or does the consequence of being hurt haunt you?

The biggest culprit behind each of these comes from fear. This floods our brains and strongly affects our minds and body. When you face a situation where you're fearful, admit it and know it's there only to teach you how to battle through.

Don't let fear overtake you. Don't allow it to dictate your life; that'll only get you trapped and victimised. Instead, learn to accept it the way it is.

Every time you run away from your fear, you give it a chance to chase you, eventually catching you up. In this rat race, the best bet is to face your fear and confront it head-on with courage and honour. Letting it thrive can make you lose faith in the Universe and detach you from your inner core.

Think of water.

Have you ever observed the flow of water? Regardless of its source, it always seeks to flow forward. Even when it sees a hindrance, it flows on to its best capability. In fact, because of its fearless flow and persistence, it even cuts through hard rock, making the impossible possible.

Enable this free reign in your life just like the natural flow of water. Break free from the clutches of fear and unveil your greatest gift locked behind it.

Ask yourself, *"What if things go exactly as planned if I dare to surpass my fears?"*

For a change, start thinking about the things that can go right instead of going wrong. The Universe will have your back no matter what.

If you're gracious enough to be open to possibilities, it might surprise you with an even better plan. Trust your abilities and this will indeed mark a huge difference in itself.

And let's say things don't go as planned; what's the worst thing that can happen? At most, you'll stay in the same circumstance you're in.

But on the contrary, imagine how great it would be if you dared to face your fear and things worked out for you. By putting yourself out there, you're being free.

Fear and its poor cousins, worry, guilt, insecurity and anxiety, will knock on our door and gives us endless excuses why we shouldn't go for something. What matters is fighting on and discovering the world beyond what awaits you.

DIY Exercise

Mention five tasks you were once fearful of but will tackle head-on today. For example, you could have the following fears:

1. Watching that dreadful super-chilling horror movie in the theatre

2. Calling that friend with whom you didn't part on the best terms

3. Sitting on that roller coaster that looked scary

4. Writing your first book, article, or poem

5. Dining alone in a crowded restaurant

Although it might look like an easy exercise, it's powerful enough to let go of your fears and trigger you to take the requisite actions. If something is stopping you from within, visualise things going right. Think of getting what you once desired. Imagine you're overcoming your inner fears.

How does this make you feel? Now, take the action you need to overcome it.

Use this space below to mention your top five:

1.

2.

3.

4.

5.

P.S: When in a place of doubt, think of a time when you were initially afraid of something, but taking the brave step led you to get what you wanted. You'd realise that being brave enough to take a step was a win in itself. Trust your gut and affirm yourself by saying:

"I am growing and learning through this process. This is an opportunity in front of me. The Universe supports and loves me."

CHAPTER TWENTY

FUELLING FORGIVENESS

Letting go of your fear and limitations is still incomplete without having forgiveness in your heart. You've weighed the baggage of pity, insecurity and guilt from your past, making you rue it time and again.

Did you face a betrayal, a breach of trust? Are you holding onto a painful memory that no longer serves its purpose other than hurting you? Met an accident? Lost someone you love?

Let's face it—we've all been there.

Look into your soul and introspect for answers deep within you.

Do you go into self-critical mode a little too much? Do you despise yourself when things don't pan out as you planned? If you've been going hard on yourself more than often, it's crucial that you begin with forgiving yourself. To gain the strength to forgive, make peace within you.

I see self-forgiveness as an art—an elusive one. By proffering a sense of inherent worth and honouring yourself as a person, you rise above your inhibitions.

Nonetheless, it gets even worse when it comes to forgive someone else who wronged you. Here are a couple of steps you can take to practice forgiving another individual:

Step 1: Know

Know what it is that you find difficult to forgive. This is the point where you accept that the damage has been done. If you have anger bubbles shooting through you, let them out; it's vital that you don't lock them inside you. Evaluate the situation and touch base with your feelings.

Step 2: Realise

From the other person's perspective, try to understand and realise why they hurt you. It might happen; it was unintentional, not directed toward you or an impersonal thing. A saying that comes to my mind now, *"Hurt people, hurt people"*. There could be a good chance that the person hurting you could come from a place of deeper hurt, worry or fear and this was a way out for them to unleash their feelings.

Step 3: Address

Is a forgiving person less difficult to be with than an unforgiving one? Of course, they are and this is what you need to address. Look for a time when you hurt someone and were forgiven by them. How did that make you feel? Now that the tables have turned, address your feelings and allow them to surface.

Step 4: Allow

Allow yourself to let go of your hard feelings. I know this isn't easy to forget and forgive something that wasn't pleasant. But this is where you allow yourself to not hold on to those negative feelings as they sweep you into a vortex of viciousness and you wouldn't want to go there. Allow yourself to forgive them; this makes you the bigger person.

Step 5: Remind

We like it or not, but finding ourselves in a situation where we need to forgive ourselves or others will come up in our lives, more often than not. It's tough to battle through these recurring events. That is when you remind yourself that you ultimately want good to prevail.

DIY Exercise

This exercise asks you to play the role of the wrongdoer and the forgiver. For this, think of the situation you're struggling to deal with. Now, begin to see it from the wrongdoer's perspective. Think from their perspective and place your point of view on the table.

Similarly, switch places and now describe your perspective as the forgiver. The whole point here is to allow yourself to surface and personally apprehend both sides of the circumstance. This exercise has a sole purpose–irrespective of the perspectives, to experience empathy and fuel forgiveness.

P.S: When you forgive, you choose to be free. And when you don't, a part of you gets stuck with anger, pain, resentment or suffering of some kind. Being stuck restricts your flow of energy; it hinders you and makes you immovable. Liberate yourself, see the abundance in life and care more to forgive, especially yourself.

WIN

CHAPTER TWENTY-ONE

READING SIGNS FROM THE UNIVERSE

The Universe constantly communicates with you, but are you paying attention to what it wants to say?

You might feel you haven't been fully aware of deciphering the "language" the Universe uses to talk to you. It could be possible that the answers you're looking for are right around you, but you can't access them due to the "language barrier."

Once you catch on to this *language*, your life experience will only grow and you'll now have answers to those questions you've been looking for your whole life.

The Universe is boundless and is a powerful force that guides, protects and heals us. All we have to do is tune in to that guidance and ask the Universe to show us the sign. Reading these signs from the Universe fuels transparent communication and shows us that we are on the right path.

But, you must actively co-create with the Universe for the communication to flow. This is where you need to flex your spiritual muscle and open yourself to the Universe. When you ask for a sign, you must also be willing to collaborate. Stay focused and release control, led by a power greater than you. Let's now look at some of the ways we can read signs from the Universe:

• **Bring more clarity**: Be clear about what you ask and want to receive. Before asking Dear Universe for a sign, be sure what you ask and what the sign would look like. Then, talk it out to the Universe about the same. When I say *talk*, I literally mean having a conversation with it in your head.

Are you baffled between two critical life choices and want the Universe to send you a sign to pick? Do you want a sign to guide you toward your best career path? Or do you simply want a sign that confirms you're on the right path in life?

Remember, clarity is crucial.

There are too many shapes, signals and signs that you might receive from the Universe. Often, recurring numbers or themes might want to pass on a message; pay attention to them.

The Universe doesn't pass on something too subtle to recognise. When a message is sent, it is always clear and loud. If you're lucky, you might receive these signs until you take the right action. Therefore, keep yourself open to receiving these signs and unlock the hidden potentials of a good life.

• **Be patient**: Without an obvious sign from the Universe that you're on the right path, patience could be annoying. But then, you mustn't manipulate the situation just to see a sign of some kind. Let it take time to get back to you with an affirmation. Better yet, let the Universe cook its magic. Until then, you can focus on trusting the process and relying on it.

• **Tune into your intuition**: The more you allow yourself to tune into your intuition, the better you carry out a conversation with the Universe. And let's say you receive a crystal-clear sign from the Universe about your ask, be decisive enough to trust it. Don't let the familiar feelings of uncertainty surface again. You already fought through it, remember?

The greatest way one can stay true to these signs is by tuning in to how you feel when you receive them. Succinctly put, if you receive a sign that says you to move forward or a validation that says you're on the right path, trust your intuition and don't second-guess it now. Dear Universe has heard you and is trying equally hard to get you what you want.

• **Give in to the Universe**: If you're looking for a sign from the Universe on a particular topic, make sure you give away your input. Don't bend the situation to meet your desire. This is the Universe's job. Completely surrender yourself to its answers and allow it to reach you naturally.

Value the experience to be more important than the answer you derive. Why do you need the Universe's help if you already have all the answers? Trust its process and you shall be fine.

• **Simplicity is the key**: The Universe loves simplicity and doesn't believe in complications. When you dwell on seeking more from a received sign, it says that you aren't into the process.

If the Universe tells you to go forward, don't hinder all the possible options such as, *"What would happen if I go in right, left or even backward?"* Keep it simple and avoid cluttering the other plausible meanings of this message at all times. The Universe is speaking and connecting to you at the moment. Let it lead your way and guide you.

P.S: Let's say you asked for a sign from the Universe and even after a significant amount of time, you still don't get a sign from it. Believe it or not, not getting a sign is a sign in itself.

For example, if you ask for a sign to know if you're in the right job and don't see a clear sign, this could mean you need to look more closely at the reasons for not working out in your career. Is the salary? Is it the culture? Is it the boss?

Note that these little breadcrumbs are meant to give us clarity and direction. Trusting the process is much needed and you'll be able to see the difference.

CHAPTER TWENTY-TWO

GIVING TO GETTING

Ever been to mountains where the child within you wanted to scream your heart out? If yes, you'd have experienced hearing back your echo, haven't you?

Whatever you scream out loud is what you hear back in multiplied versions–the last voice being much fainter than the first one. And the more you scream, your echo reverts louder.

The Universe works similarly. If you scream *"I want more money"* to the Universe, it calls back with *"I want more money"*. If you scream, *"I want more love,"* it calls back with *"I want more love."*

If you command it to the Universe to gift you something, the Universe finds it too technical to decode. You can't win just by screaming. The more you want, the more it wants too.

When you say, *"I want to give,"* the Universe responds with, *"I want to give back to you with interest."* The beauty of the Universe is that it gives without any expectations. When you let go of malicious attachments such as greed and desperation, the Universe gets the message and gives back unconditionally.

Long story short, to give is to get.

The more you give respect, the greater you get back with it. The more you give love, the greater you get back with it, and so on.

That is what the law of nature entails; the more you give to Mother Nature, it returns unfailingly. Part with what you wish to get, and see the magic.

To manifest abundance, giving is necessary. The more you give to others, the higher you receive.

Let's assume you say to the Universe, *"I am not happy with my salary; I want you to give me more of it,"* or, *"My boss does not appreciate me. Hence I want you to give me appreciation."*

You tell the Universe that you don't have something through these messages. You indicate to the Universe, *"I don't have enough and that is why I can't give."* Then, the Universe has no choice but to support your belief that you don't have enough to give.

Therefore, give, without any strings attached, without any expectation and any conditions. Only then will you be able to relish the pure joy of giving.

If you're already in an abundance of money, give it to the people who are in need or are less fortunate than you. Charity can always be your go-to.

When you give, you naturally fall into a state of abundance. Remember, giving doesn't always have to carry a financial annotation.

It's not always money that you can pass on to one another. There are so many things other than money that you can give, such as respect, appreciation, love, support and even time!

If you don't want to fill anyone's wallet with money, at least fill their heart with compassion. The Universe doesn't need your money. It runs on integrity and love. When you do your part, the Universe meets you halfway and does its part.

You become worthy of getting back when you give, that too, in abundance.

When you give, the law of attraction gets this hint and starts working toward your dream.

When you give, you become selfless and light, which the Universe adores.

DIY Exercise

What are some of the causes that you're truly passionate about? There could be many causes around you that could be upsetting and you'd like to do something to curb them. The world battles with illiteracy, and there is a severe shortage of food and water for people; women still face and deal with several safety-related issues. Pick a cause you truly want to see transformed and find something that motivates you to take a step further.

For example, if you like playing with kids, you might consider taking a tour of a nearby orphanage and spending some quality time with those kids if that is what makes you happy. If you want to do something for the nursing homes, you can shed a small portion of your salary as a donation for their welfare.

Or, if none of these appeals to you, you can spend a day mentoring someone with something that you're proficient at. For example, I coach and mentor students in my circle regarding writing and help them get started.

Look around you; limitless opportunities are beckoning you.

Sometimes, even the smallest gestures make a profound impact. Giving away your seat to a pregnant lady on the train, applauding the struggling magician on the road, or even holding the door for someone carrying loads of stuff.

What truly matters is that you're giving, and better yet, giving without any attached conditions.

P.S: Nothing beats generosity and kindness. Even a random act of goodwill today will bring a difference to the way you feel. When you appreciate the value of everything around you, you tend to see life in an even more beautiful light.

With whatever you have, you are powerful to give.

CHAPTER TWENTY-THREE

LIVING IN THE 'NOW'

From parents to our yoga instructors to even our textbooks, we hear this phrase: to live in the present or the 'now'. But they don't tell you why it is so important to love the present and what you are missing out on by not doing so.

We all have something or the other that we'd like to change from our past, had we a magic wand. We tend to spend most of our time regretting, repenting and ruing the things that didn't go well in our pasts, something that we failed to achieve and say, *"I wish it were possible to travel back in time to change ...."*

You're done berating yourself for what had happened, crying over spilt milk and feeling sorry for yourself.

Now, let's run you through what happens when you don't live in the present. To begin with, your mind starts wandering off to places, fretting about things you could have or couldn't have done in the past. Above anything, it distracts you from what you have with you right now.

Bygone is bygone.

Worrying about the past is redundant and will never come to fruition. In fact, spending a second's worth of time thinking about the past is wasting your time.

Manifesting is all about your belief in yourself and your dreams–a belief that you're going to make your dream come true. When you stay in the present, you give your all, paving a bigger road for your wishes to transform into reality.

When was the last time you smelled the fragrance of a flower? How does it feel when you're sun-kissed early morning? How about the smell of fresh soil after it rains?

Did you take a moment to live in these everyday scenarios and appreciate the beautiful little things?

We don't take pleasure in the small things of life. We ignore what we have right around us in our very present and dwell over the past.

Of course, money can buy many things, but it can't buy many more. As they say, *"The most beautiful things in the world are free."*

Ensure that whenever you encounter a thing of beauty, you relish and take it all in. Try avoiding things that fall under the 'materialistic' world.

As humans, we tend to realise the worth of something only after we lose it or no longer have access to it. Some of which are so priceless that the power of money can't buy.

Learn to look rather than see.

Learn to listen rather than to hear.

Even though these words are interchangeably used, they differ significantly in their meanings and usage.

Start living each moment from now on to its fullest potential. Give your all to your present and fill it with attention. Recognise the fact that every moment is unique and you've allowed making the most out of it.

Seize the deal.

Unleash the baggage you've been carrying your whole life–shame, guilt, remorse. When you embrace the present, you enjoy a sense of satisfaction–an unmatched feeling.

Now, you might be wondering what I can do to feel more 'at the moment'. Here are a few tips to get started:

How do you start your day? A question you've already dealt with at the beginning of this book?

I take a moment to visualise how I would like to see my day go. It's like a little choreography in my head. But when I do that, it helps me focus, retain these visualisations and navigate through my day seamlessly.

For example, if you're working on a particular project today, say, designing a gown, mapping an architectural sheet, or developing an application, ensure you don't get distracted easily.

Have complete attention to your task. Stay in the present and think of ways how you can make this project bigger and better.

Stop worrying about what can go wrong in your project. Instead, fixate more on creative ideas and systematically plan them.

- Say no to multi-tasks at all times. I find people claiming, *"I'm good at multi-tasking. I can cook and clean the garden while dropping my son off to school at the same time"*.

Do you go for a brisk jog alone, or are you accompanied by your phone?

Do you enjoy a nice hot meal, or are you accompanied by your favourite show on your TV?

Do one thing at one time and give it your all. When going out for a jog, focus just on your jog. Likewise for your meals too.

- Practise digital detox. You don't have to be in your inbox every second of every day. Take a break from your back-to-back meetings. To see who commented on your latest picture on Facebook can wait. To check whether someone slid into your IG'S DMs can wait too. It's time to tune into yourself and soak in the present.
- Avoid procrastination: Even if you can't follow up with the first and second points, please ensure you follow this.

I see people around me who procrastinate for a living and claim to be professional procrastinators. While getting lost in vagueness is still fine, we mustn't be enslaved by it. When we procrastinate, we give our minds a hint that we're ideal and you already know, *"An ideal mind is a ...."*

Now that you got it right, let's get you into a DIY exercise to get the most out of your potential.

DIY Exercise

If it is possible in your circle and if you have the time, get out of your room today and connect with an older person.

They could be someone from your apartment, someone you met on the street last week, or your grandparents too!

Ask them what is life. What is it that life has taught them? What did they enjoy the most in life? Do they have any regrets? What did they do to cope with it? How would they do it if given an opportunity to re-do whatever they regret?

Observe their eyes, body language and tone when they answer these questions.

Now rewind to ask yourself, *"What would you want to feel like when you grow old?"*

By ultimately experiencing and living lives to the fullest, we have the power to enjoy a holistic life and attain satisfaction.

P.S: Make a decisive choice to be happy from this moment onwards. When you live in the present, you touch the source of life. Thus, remember to smile. Take care of your body. Pamper yourself. Treat yourself well.

CHAPTER TWENTY-FOUR

DESERVING WORTHINESS

Answer this:

"Am I worthy and do I deserve happiness"?

You might wonder, what kind of a question is that? Of course, I'm worthy enough to deserve happiness.

While we might say so, we often might not feel so. The extent to which we don't feel worthy or deserving varies significantly from person to person. To feel so at all times will be something that most people grapple with.

This begins with a myth that you have to praise, hail, or worship the Universe for it to recognise your efforts. Unless you haven't received a stamp of proof from the Universe that you're worthy, you don't seem to admit it the easy way that you're worthy by default. Our fundamental human nature makes us believe, *"I must prove my worth to the Universe to reach my dream."*

Truth being told, the Universe adores you and knows you're deserving even if you don't do anything. It's time for you to believe the same and know that there is no dearth of goodness around you.

Say this sentence out loud:

"My very existence makes me worthy and deserving."

When you say these words, you step into the experience of contributing to your role as a powerful creator. This gives you the confidence to get all you once aspired for: happiness, a purpose and overall emotional goodness.

Realign your perspective in a way that your self-doubt about your worth vanishes. As you realign, you'll gain the confidence to validate your newfound belief and enhance how you feel now.

When these feelings soak into you, you'll have the strength to no longer wander about the inane questions; of what or what don't you deserve. Purely realising your worth will enable your former feelings to transform into merriment.

Start viewing your life from a fresh, positive lens which helps you reform how you think and see perspectives.

Know that kindness goes a long way. Be that person who compliments a complete stranger on the road or the one who accompanies a colleague for lunch on their first day at work.

Believe in the following statements:

"I am here to offer positivity, happiness, confidence, and joy to the people around me."

"I promote to people's well-being as much as they do to me."

"I strive to bring ease and comfort wherever I go."

Nonetheless, there still can be times when you engage in self-sabotage or self-critic thought that could question whether you can do this. Flying from the rigid ideas you once had about your worth to finding solace within yourself can take a toll on you at first.

This starts with you. Love yourself and know that you deserve well. Adding certain habits to your routine that make you care more for your mental, physical and emotional being–something that proves that you're worthy and you deserve nothing short of the best.

Act first, and then worthiness will follow.

And when I say act, it doesn't have to be anything 007, James Bond-ish. It can be something as simple as taking a nice hot bubble bath. If volunteering for an old age centre makes you feel worthy, have at it. If splurging at some spa, treating yourself to some manicure, or even a haircut makes you feel happy, have a go at them too.

And when you cultivate these habits, you'll begin to feel lighter, happier and better. With this, you welcome an upgraded version of yourself—confident, revitalised and cheerful. You finally gain a sense of worthiness you never thought you had access to. This lands you in a purely magnetic frequency, enticing the Universe to recognise your conditioned efforts.

And just feeling joyful from all of this helps you radiate a higher frequency than the Universe connects to, thereby elevating your happiness to knock on your door, time and again.

DIY Exercise

This should be the easiest DIY exercise in this book. This is when you're going to do something that makes you feel special, worthy and deserving. For example, pick an activity that gives you a sense of satisfaction.

It could also be learning a new skill you always wanted but never had the time to. If not, pick a few of your strengths that you'd like to refine. Are you good at solving a Rubik's cube? Try to hone your timings and when you're through, don't forget to reward yourself when you achieve something big.

And if none of these work for you, dress the best you can for an event, a party or an occasion that is coming up on your calendar. Be it a date, a meeting with a friend after years or if you just have a much-awaited festival around the corner, dress up. Take pride in your appearance and you'll start to feel the difference just by the way you dress. This is the change that you need to see and cherish.

P.S: Trust the nuances of these activities. Trust the process. Believe that you're worthy and deserving, come what may, no matter how much your mind might fight you on that. It's a battle in your head that you can totally win. It's about shifting that focus to the point where you break free from the dubiousness and trust your worth.

CHAPTER TWENTY-FIVE

You're Manifesting-Ready

Congratulations, this welcomes you to the last chapter of this book.

You're all set to manifest the life of your dreams. Whatever you've wanted–your dream job, a magnificent house, a loving spouse or winning that contest–is here. The wait is over. Take your position, unfurl your wings and fly. The Universe has heard you. You're ready!

It's time!

It's time for your efforts, hard work, dedication and passion for wreathing into a new 'you.' It's time to gear up and receive what you've been keeping away from.

You've learned to overcome every difficulty that comes your way. You have the answers to life that you once were unaware of. You know that treating yourself with umpteen love, respect and kindness is what you've always deserved. You know that it's you who has the power to sculpt your reality and gift yourself the life you had always dreamt of.

Now, you'll be able to smell the first blissful petrichor of the rain. Now, you have the courage to take some time off and visit your dream destination that you hovered for long in hopes of finding the perfect time. Now, you'll also realise that there is always a presence of goodness in everything around you. In short, now is when you put everything this book has taught you into fair practice.

When you give yourself a genuine chance to change how your life has been so far, you give a heads up to the Universe that you're ready to immerse into life's bright, cheerful and amazing side.

Acknowledge that you're divine and are connected to anything and everything around you. Embrace the truth that great things are coming into your life.

Break free from the pondering thoughts about what and why you can't do something. Tell the Universe that you're prepared to accept your new and better reality and know it's possible.

You are powerful and have always been!

All that you have ever imagined and wished for is right before you. And it is easier than imagined to grab and make it yours. A heart filled with gratitude is what it takes for the the Universe to offer you more of it.

The Universe adores you no matter how many mistakes you make or what you think of yourself. Give away the fitting instructions and place your order. Believe that greater things are coming your way. Let it in.

You're journey begins,
You're the best,
You're manifesting-ready!

Conclusion

The simplicity in being you, embracing love and manifesting from your heart is inspiring in itself—that's all this book is about.

What if you were chosen to read this book?

What if you didn't stumble upon this book coincidentally and it was a sign from above to have your hands on it to learn from?

What if these were concurrences and you're a step closer to manifesting the life of your dreams with the help of this book?

What if this was the Universe's way of letting you know that you're undoubtedly powerful, the world is full of endless possibilities and that you've been chosen to manifest abundancies?

Rely on and trust the prescribed techniques in this book. Grow and uncover potential within you. Live every day like a new opportunity to explore and discover the goodness of the world around you.

The only thing that you need to keep in mind and essentially prioritise while reading this book is *"you."*

Place yourself in every instance, example, and exercise of this book and accept that it was exclusively meant for you.

As much as you love expansion and possibility, the Universe loves them and loves you as well.

There is yet so much left in the world for you to watch, revel in and fall in love with.

Your dreams are within your reach and each of your manifestations can come true, no matter how impossible they seem at first.

Get ready to hop on this roller coaster and enjoy your ride.

The best time to start running toward your dreams is *now*.

There is no better time. Push your 'start' button and master your life.

Speaking the language of the Universe just got easier!